1492
And All That

ROBERT ROYAL is vice president and Olin Fellow in Religion and Society at the Ethics and Public Policy Center. He has taught at Brown University, Rhode Island College, and The Catholic University of America, and was a Fulbright Scholar in Italy. From 1980 to 1982, he was editor-in-chief of *Prospect* magazine in Princeton, New Jersey. Among the books he has published are *A Century of Catholic Social Thought* (co-editor, with George Weigel), *Crisis and Opportunity: U.S. Policy in Central America and the Caribbean* (co-editor, with Mark Falcoff), and, with Virgil Nemoianu, *Play, Literature, Religion: Essays in Cultural Intertextuality*. His articles have appeared in numerous publications, including the *Washington Post*, the *Washington Times*, *National Review*, *The American Spectator*, *First Things*, and *Crisis*.

1492
And All That

*Political Manipulations
of History*

ROBERT ROYAL

ETHICS AND PUBLIC POLICY CENTER

Library of Congress Cataloging-in-Publication Data

Royal, Robert, 1949–
1492 and all that ; political manipulations of history / Robert Royal.
p. cm.
Includes bibliographical references and index.
1. Columbus, Christopher.   2. America—Discovery and exploration—Spanish.   3. America—Discovery and explora-tion—Spanish—Historiography.   4. Indians—First contact with Europeans.   5. Indians—First contact with Europeans—Historiography.   6. Pluralism (Social sciences)—America.
7. Pluralism (Social sciences)—America—Historiography.
I. Title.
E118.R69   1992
970.01'1'072—dc20   92–22946 CIP

ISBN 0–89633–174–1 (cloth : alk. paper)

Distributed by
National Book Network
4720 Boston Way
Lanham, MD 20706

3 Henrietta Street
London WC2E 8LU England

All Ethics and Public Policy Center books are produced on acid-free paper. The paper used in this publication meets the minimum requirements of American National Standard for Information Sciences—Permanence of Paper for Printed Library Materials, ANSI Z39.48–1984.   ♾™

Ethics and Public Policy Center
1015 Fifteenth Street N.W.
Washington, D.C. 20005
(202) 682–1200

Venient annis
Saecula seris, quibus Oceanus
Vincula rerum laxent, et ingens
Pateat tellus, Typhisque novos
Detegat Orbes, nec sit terris
Ultima Thule.
                    —Seneca

The day was 4-Flower and the year 1-House.
They perished and all the mountains
    perished with them.
The water lasted fifty-two years
    and then their years ended.
We are now in the Sun 4-Movement
    and under this Sun
There will be earthquakes and famine,
And we shall all be destroyed.

                    —*Nahuatl Legend*
                    of the Suns

Contents

Acknowledgments

Properly to acknowledge those who have contributed to this book would be a lengthy task. I can mention here only the most central persons. Veronica, Elizabeth, John Paul, and Natalie Royal were wonderfully understanding and patient with the often absent and even more often distracted author. George Weigel, president of the Ethics and Public Policy Center, provided, as is his wont, encouragement and enthusiasm throughout the project. Gretchen Baudhuin assisted at every stage in the research and bravely endured many of the arguments when they were still in oral form. Jacqueline Stark was a model editor who helped me to clarify the text and my mind on a number of points. Some of these pages appeared in different form in that remarkable journal *First Things*; I am grateful to its editors, Richard John Neuhaus and James Neuchterlein, for invitations to write articles that dovetailed nicely with the developing book. Finally, Bartholomew de la Torre, O.P., with whom I have had the pleasure of climbing both the Pyramid of the Sun in Teotihuacán and the shrine of Our Lady of Guadalupe at Tepeyac, has over many years demonstrated to me by word and personal example that the melding of indigenous and European cultures in the New World continues to bear fruit.

ROBERT ROYAL
May 15, 1992

ix

Introduction

In the highest literary achievements of both Western and non-Western cultures, human history is often viewed through lenses combining national epic and personal tragedy. Texts as diverse as Virgil's *Aeneid* and the Hindu sacred poem *Bhagavad Gita* portray crucial events of the past—indeed, foundational historic battles, acknowledged to have produced much good in the present—as inextricably bound up with painful choices and morally worrisome violence. In the battle that will ensure the founding of Rome, Aeneas, after a moment spent agonizing over whether to spare Turnus, sees that the opposing warrior is wearing a belt captured from a slain comrade and kills him in the last lines of the epic; before a crucial clash that will determine the future of India, Arjuna, in anguish over the need to do battle with beloved teachers, friends, and members of his own family, ultimately obeys the counsel of the god Krishna and goes to war. The glory of Rome and the splendor of India, as their own high cultures recognized, were rooted—as are all large-scale human endeavors—in human loss, contradictions, and moral doubt, for which Virgil invented the immortal phrase *lacrimae rerum*.

Among the peoples of the Americas, perhaps the Mexicans, whose high indigenous cultures already possessed their own epics and tragic songs, have best preserved this sense of the epic and tragic dimensions of sweeping historical change. The conquest of the Aztecs by the Spanish under Cortés did not simply replace one people and culture with another, as is often assumed. From the heroism, brutality, courage, and turmoil of that era—from the

1

colossal confluence of Aztec and Spaniard—something new emerged: Mexicans. Appropriately, Mexico celebrates October 12 not as Columbus Day but as *el día de la raza*, "the day of the race," the new people of mixed Native American and European heritage.

In the United States we are usually distrustful of grand epic visions and reluctant to accept human tragedy, both of which we would like to think belong to the bad, old, striving, and overreaching worlds left behind by our immigrant ancestors. We prefer to see American life as a perpetually fresh start—without, or at least beyond, history—that provides us with the opportunity to do or to become whatever we decide upon, ancient human limitations notwithstanding. The American story, in this view, is the story of a New World in several mutually reinforcing senses. Not only are we different from the Old World geographically, we hope we are different spiritually as well. We do not accept Europe's somewhat cynical expectations of government and society. As Luigi Barzini, a shrewd and sympathetic outside observer, once noticed, the founding documents of the United States show that even perfection is not enough for us. We seek a "more perfect union . . . immediately, today, tomorrow morning at the latest."[1] What other nation would have designated itself a *novus ordo seclorum*?

This drive for perfection and for deliverance from history has produced many of the most characteristically American achievements and is, for good and bad, a continuing American legacy. Yet as time has passed and American history has lengthened, the epic and the tragic, which sooner or later take their places as part of human life, have emerged to trouble the New World story. As Gibbon rightly said, history *per se* is "a long tale of crimes and follies." Anticipating the quincentenary of Columbus's arrival in these lands, diverse voices have arisen to assert, on the one hand, the epic grandeur of the European migration and, on the other, the tragic consequences of that expansion for native peoples, for Africans imported as slaves, and for nature itself. Though other nations have their disputes about the meaning of October 12, 1992, in the United States that date swings sharply between outright celebration and outright condemnation.

INTRODUCTION

In a culture that has long denied epic and tragedy, both praise and blame quickly become ultimate weapons. For the critics, who often give the impression of having just discovered some of the unfortunate, violent, but long-known facts of the American past, the presence of evil in the historical record totally discredits the myth of American exceptionalism and of the United States as a just society. These critics charge that Americans have hypocritically disavowed the unsavory parts of their own past to protect a self-righteous, sanitized national story.

For many defenders, who frequently seem to regard any criticism of the United States as a prelude to total denunciation, admitting the tragic dimension of America's past threatens to obliterate the distinctive character of our history. Because so much of what tenuously binds together Americans of widely diverse backgrounds hinges on American ideals of liberty and justice for all, these defenders believe that serious criticism based on real American events may upset the entire national applecart. They point to the basic decency of modern-day America and suspect— not entirely wrongly—that many contemporary critics of the American past are really pursuing an agenda for the American present.

But radical critics and wholesale defenders of the American experiment in fact pay subconscious homage to an abiding New World myth. As the historian David Noble has argued: "a central tradition in American historical writing has been the assumption that the United States, unlike the European nations, has a covenant that makes Americans a chosen people who have escaped from the terror of historical change to live in timeless harmony with nature."[2] The fundamental point of contention between the two warring parties is whether we possessed that "timeless harmony" in the past or can achieve it in the future. Popular attitudes often mirror this historical perspective. Americans tend to think of their country in terms of a basic human perfection, and bridle—either in criticism or defense—at any evidence that the United States is, or should be, just another nation in the history of the human race.

The present volume makes no claims to Olympian objectivity

3

nor does it seek to conceal its own judgments. It does not even aspire to be comprehensive history. Probably no one alive knows enough to write the full story of European and native peoples either during or after the earliest period of contact—though many current commentators have had the hubris to attempt it. While this volume presumes that the United States is overwhelmingly a great good place now, it does not attempt to ignore or underplay the tragedy of its origins and development, nor its continuing problems. And entering, as it does, an already polemicized debate, it cannot help but reply to arguments that have come to dominate the public discussion.

Since the Civil War we have become an indissolubly united nation, but our sense of the epic heroism and the tragic costs, for North and South, that secured that unity has grown progressively weaker as the benefits of American civilization have come to be taken for granted. The unanticipated success of Ken Burns's 1991 PBS television series "The Civil War" shows that Americans are capable of taking to heart the wrenching emotions produced by such conflicts. As we approach 1992, it would be useful to recover, in similar fashion, a just sense of both the glory and the agony that attended the arrival of Europeans on this continent.

To anticipate one possible misconception: invoking the epic and tragic is not a way of using artificial literary categories to gain political and moral absolution for the past or the present. Rather, these concepts exist precisely because they reflect a deep and valid understanding of some permanent elements of human life. For example, the isolation of the Americas from the other continents for thousands of years prior to 1492 left native populations tragically helpless before diseases that arrived from abroad. Whether Europeans, Asians, or Africans had made the first trip linking these shores to the rest of the world, millions of deaths were poised to occur solely because of geographical accidents. Furthermore, while we must never lose sight of universal moral principles and judgments, we also need a solid sense of the ways in which those principles may clash with one another or become entangled in concrete circumstances. Tragedy, as we know from Greek

4

drama, is not solely occupied with the triumph of evil over good, or one evil over another. Tragedy is probably sharpest when the situation dictates that a choice be made between incompatible goods leading to the unavoidable loss of something humanly valuable. Even in epic achievements human costs inevitably must be paid. Epic and tragedy do not conceal truth beneath artificiality but open windows onto a fuller reality.

Toward that same end this book concentrates mainly on a range of moral questions about the European settlement of the Americas. In doing so, it necessarily also tries to get some facts straight that have become distorted by polemics. In the approach to 1992, many books have already been written to show the depravity of the Europeans and the purity of the native peoples. Some readers may think this book attempts the contrary. But instead of using Renaissance Europe or neolithic indigenous societies as a stick with which to beat the present, this brief study aims at examining what happened when widely divergent cultures—each with its share of humane individuals and cultural riches, as well as ruthless tyrants and cultural monstrosities—met and mingled.

Disentangling the various strands of this process is both complicated and subject to dispute at every point. Some disproportion also results from the fact that, with few exceptions, indigenous peoples left no written records. Not only did the victors write the history, for a long time they were the only ones who *could* write the history. But the evidence we are fortunate enough to have seems to confirm that little of the cultural mixing in the Americas can be characterized in the strictly black-and-white terms usually applied to it by various factions. Discrete events were certainly at times horrifying evils; other events show human interaction of a gratifying sort not usually encountered in everyday life; still others show unprecedented situations demanding—but only rarely getting—heroic human solutions. The most important methodological issue here, however, is to see the original record as a reality in its own time and not to succumb, as far as is humanly possible, to the temptation to let contemporary issues crush fragile historical truths. There are dishonorable episodes that will always be a part of the American past. Our duty now is to make sure that in fleeing one type of dishonor, we do not rush headlong into another.

I am fully aware that this approach may satisfy no one but me. It is one of the major premises of this book, however, that there are various forms of imperialism. And none, perhaps, is so insidious as the imperialism that tries to defend some portion of the past at the cost of distorting it to satisfy the imperious, and seemingly noble, emotions of the present. Whatever their flaws or accomplishments, the Europeans and native peoples who first met and began the process in which we are now all living at least deserve to be understood in their own fullness. When we make them over into our own image and likeness, or redefine them in contemporary terms, we *use* other human beings, now dead, rather than working, as we should, to *understand* them.

Only when we have far more of the story straight, and are at ease in facing a non-idealized America with a concrete history, will it be appropriate to take stock of what has happened in the past—and to seek to draw some lessons from it for our collective and common future.

NOTE: The very terms American, indigenous, Native American, Indian, and European, as well as many others, have been drawn into the intellectual and political turmoil over 1492. The use of these terms in this text is governed by the intention to give no deliberate offense to any person—or to the English language.

1

Myths and Anti-Myths

The greatest event since the creation of the world (excluding the incarnation and death of Him who created it) is the discovery of the Indies.

—Francisco López de Gómara
Historia General (1552)[1]

Of the many symbolic dates that have been suggested for the birth of the modern world, one of the strongest candidates is 1492. Depending on what we mean by modern, of course, a case could also be made for the Renaissance, the Reformation, the Industrial or French Revolutions, the outbreak of the First World War, the confirmation of Einstein's theory of relativity, the dropping of the atom bomb on Japan, or several other events as being *the* turning point towards modernity. But events of that magnitude and kind—political, religious, military, scientific—have occurred around the globe during the tens of thousands of years of human history. If by modern, however, we mean the human space in which we now find ourselves, one world in which the entire earth with all its peoples and cultures and technologies has become a single, if tangled, social complex, and in which any event anywhere has importance for the whole species *homo sapiens*, then 1492 stands unrivaled as the pivotal year for the birth of the modern world.

Such large-scale speculations are far from idle when we try to evaluate Columbus's first voyages. Since the very concept of the "world" as we know it depends on what happened in 1492, many

7

more issues come into play in our assessments than the bare historical events. In a sense, the past five hundred years also come under scrutiny because various continuities and developments directly link 1492 with our own time. Most visibly, contact between the Old World and the New World radically changed flora and fauna—and therefore attitudes towards the environment—for both; affected population and mortality through war, disease, agriculture, and settlement patterns; and revolutionized European as well as Native American thought and culture. All these factors have had profound effects on the shape of the modern world.[2]

They also have introduced some uncertainties about how we should conduct ourselves during the Columbus quincentenary, particularly since in 1992 we are uncertain about so much else in American life. For the most part, professional historians have continued to do what they have done for decades, pointing out good and bad consequences of Europe's role in linking the Americas with the Old World and in creating the first true global networks. Scholarly knowledge about the several peoples involved in this monumental saga is more detailed and set in better perspective than at any time in the five hundred years since Columbus. But knowledge alone is not shaping current interpretations. A substantial group of historians and political actors have entered the public arena seeking to use the Columbus anniversary as a springboard for advancing political agendas.

Earlier Political Distortions

This has happened before. In fact, it has been a persistent feature of the Columbus story since the very beginning of American history. Columbus's scholarly son, Fernando, wrote one of the earliest accounts of his father's exploits. Following Columbus's own lead, Fernando portrays him as a lone genius opposed by dark enemies and scoffers. Sailing routes were the hi-tech commercial secrets of the fifteenth century, and many of Columbus's texts deliberately conceal information that he does not wish to pass into the hands of others. Furthermore, Columbus was not above coloring the truth, to say nothing of lying, to protect and advance his claims on the Spanish monarchs. In an age where vast distances, slow communications, and new human complexities hampered government and oversight, it was perhaps understandable that he would also try—after the fact—to elaborate justifications for actions he had taken out of necessity and in the face of unprecedented circumstances.

Columbus, as will become clear in the next chapter, was an astonishing sailor, perhaps one of the greatest in all history. He knew how to keep a crew in line on ship, but as a governor on *terra firma*, he was little better than disastrous in any but the most favorable circumstances. His third voyage ended with his being returned to Europe in chains and with the Spanish monarchs forbidding him to return to Hispaniola, the advanced base for exploration in the Americas, because of the ill feeling that had arisen toward him there among the Spaniards. When he was shipwrecked and marooned on Jamaica for over a year on his fourth and final voyage, he faced various temporary mutinies before being rescued. By the end of his life, Columbus would be entangled in acrimonious legal battles over his rights in the Indies. Some Spaniards thought he had misrepresented the ease with which wealth might be acquired in the New World; others accused him of nepotism and highhandedness toward Europeans on the island of Hispaniola. It is no wonder, then, that in 1592 the one-hundredth anniversary of his first voyage went largely uncelebrated. Columbus's real-life political disputes had to fade before he could emerge as a symbolic figure in the myth of America.

In 1692 his star still had not risen. But by 1792 his historical fortunes, owing to circumstances in the New World, were poised to explode. North America, growing in wealth and liberty, had just thrown off the yoke of George III. Reflecting the atmosphere of the time, Kings College in New York, founded in 1754, renamed itself Columbia. Unhampered by much close knowledge of Columbus's life, several prominent Americans, including Ben Franklin, saw in the explorer a predecessor on the road to liberty, the initiator of an American spirit distinct from that of the old

Europe. The new capital of the United States was named the District of Columbia. Some zealous partisans of liberty had even wanted to name the new nation after Columbus.

And by 1892, the four-hundredth anniversary of his first voyage to the New World, Columbus had for most people in this country been transformed into the precursor of a confident and progressive United States of America. Preparations for the official celebration, the Columbian Exhibition in Chicago, were so elaborate, in fact, that the program did not get into full swing until 1893. The opening proclaimed 1492 not merely a historical date but a turning point in the emancipation of mankind. Though Native American groups staged some protests and some scholarly criticism[3] of him as a sailor and a man appeared even at that point—Columbus's historical high tide—Columbus had largely become a myth serving several political and intellectual agendas and some popular uses.[4]

The motives behind this apotheosis were quite straightforward and understandable. America was in an expansive mood, and Columbus was a useful symbol of enterprise and liberty—and not only for establishment WASPs. Italian-Americans, for example, looking for an opportunity to display their contributions to a then mostly unwelcoming American culture, erected a statue to Columbus in New York in what is still Columbus Circle. A decade earlier, some American Catholics, mostly Irish, had founded the Knights of Columbus both to strengthen ethnic identity and to hold up the navigator as a model for those who wanted to become better Catholics and better citizens. Despite the self-interest and elementary historical knowledge that went into them, these initiatives did have the virtue of pointing out the Mediterranean and Catholic contributions to an America that had lost sight of them.

The Vatican, too, found in the fourth centenary a historical opportunity. In the 1870s a French count, Roselly de Lorgues, had proposed Columbus for sainthood, a cause later taken up by such distinguished French literary figures as Léon Bloy and Paul Claudel.[5] The First Vatican Council rejected that proposal "on moral grounds," probably because of Columbus's long liaison with

Beatriz de Arana, the mother of his illegitimate son Fernando. (At the time sensitivity to the admiral's alleged misdeeds in the New World was not very high.) In 1892, however, Pope Leo XIII did issue an encyclical praising Columbus, *Quarto abeunte saeculo*. While this document keeps Columbus separate from the saints, who have superhuman virtues, it does praise him for virtues of another kind: "For the exploit is in itself the highest and grandest which any age has ever seen accomplished by man; and he who achieved it, for the greatness of mind and heart, can be compared to but few in the history of humanity."[6] Leo allows that Columbus sought personal gain and glory, but believed, as did many people in the nineteenth century, that ambition was often a spur to achievement. Columbus's most monumental feat, however, was carried out under divine inspiration: he brought Christianity to "a mighty multitude, cloaked in miserable darkness, given over to evil rites, and the superstitious worship of vain gods." Columbus's opening up of new mission territory also compensated for some of the losses the Church was about to suffer because of the Protestant Reformation.

All the popular late-nineteenth-century views of Columbus, even the Vatican's, stemmed directly from progressive ideologies, and produced, as well as drew strength from, remarkable misrepresentations of history. We have all heard it vaguely claimed, for instance, that Christopher Columbus proved to a disbelieving and dark, late-medieval Europe that the world was not flat. Jeffrey Burton Russell, a medieval historian, has recently assembled evidence exploding this and several other historical myths that have been attached to Columbus since the nineteenth century.[7] Russell shows beyond dispute that any educated person in late-medieval Europe already knew, as did the ancient Greco-Roman world, that the earth was spherical. Nineteenth-century historians simply invented a progressive-Columbus myth for several reasons. Some hated the Spanish Empire and Roman Catholicism. Others wanted to demonstrate the superiority of the modern world in general, and America in particular, to all earlier ages. Still others found it expedient to portray religion, particularly Christianity, as a reactionary force and an opponent of enlightenment.

The Flat Error

How was what Russell calls the "Flat Error" introduced? The answer to this question is instructive, especially if we wish to be on guard against distortions that our current proclivities may inject into new historical interpretations. Ironically, the process began as what appeared to be a much-needed scholarly revision of history.

Only two ancient Christian writers of any significance put forward a flat-earth theory: Lactantius (ca.245–325), a Latin convert whose views antedated the sophisticated hermeneutics of Church Fathers like Saint Augustine and Saint John Chrysostom and propounded a crude "biblical" cosmos; and Cosmas Indicopleustes, a Greek who, writing around 547–49, argued that the universe was a vaulted arch with the earth as its floor. Lactantius was posthumously condemned as a heretic, and Cosmas was and is so obscure that a student may easily complete a graduate degree in medieval studies without ever coming across his name. Of further importance in the present context is the fact that Cosmas was unknown to western Europe until 1706 and could have had no influence in Columbus's time.

As anyone who has read *The Divine Comedy* will recall, Dante takes for granted a spherical earth and a Ptolemaic universe, in fact makes them of major structural significance in his poem. All other serious medieval thinkers held the same belief. How, then, did their views get steam-rollered into the Flat Error? (A "Wizard of Id" cartoon included among the illustrations to Russell's volume shows a mock-Solomonic king reconciling a dispute between the court's flat partisans and round partisans by proclaiming that the world is both flat and round: "I call it the Pizza Theory.") Russell points to two main schools of revisionist historians as the primary culprits: the progressives of the early nineteenth century and the

Darwinians after 1870. Both groups had an interest in revising the record for contemporary purposes.

The Nineteenth-Century Columbus: Protestant and Progressive

Washington Irving, probably the best known of the progressives, concocted an image of Columbus as a modern man who had freed himself from the constraints of feudal and Catholic Europe to help create the democratic and Protestant New World. During a stay in Spain, Irving had read some of the original archival materials on Columbus, and he selected from them to make of that Catholic Genoese navigator the unlikely hero of American Protestantism and progressivism. Irving's *History of the Life and Voyages of Columbus*—a vivid, romanticized, dramatic, and often fictitious moral tale—was published in 1837.[8] Despite its shortcomings as truth, the book set the tone of most studies and popular beliefs about the explorer for the rest of the century and, in some crucial ways, beyond.

Exploration in Columbus's time essentially called for state backing. Columbus's failure to gain support from the leading maritime explorers of his day, the Portuguese, and his subsequent difficulties in convincing Ferdinand and Isabella, king and queen of the newly united kingdom of Spain, are well known. His troubles stemmed in no small degree from the fact that learned opinion in his time held that the world was larger than Columbus thought and the landmasses smaller, which would mean a long open-water distance from Europe to Cathay. The Spanish monarchs even called together a few learned churchmen, some from the University of Salamanca, who were also skilled astronomers and geographers, to evaluate Columbus's project. It appears they recommended against it but out of knowledge, not superstition.[9]

In Washington Irving's "history," however, this judgment is shown to have all the trappings of the fanaticism and obscurantism once facilely ascribed to everything "medieval." And in the work of a host of later self-styled progressive writers, the Inquisition and "monastic bigotry" take on life as symbolic forces that must

13

be overcome to create America. Irving transformed the persons consulted by the crown into a formal council of "learned" theologians who confronted Columbus with a passage from—Lactantius! A textbook in 1880 paraphrases Irving's scene: "Is there anyone so foolish as to believe that there are people living on the other side of the earth with their heels upward and their heads hanging down?"[10]

Though, as was mentioned earlier, Lactantius had been declared heretical over a thousand years earlier, modern historical ignorance and arrogance made it an easy step to the kind of truth-versus-heresy morality play that has persisted even as late as this exchange in Joseph Chiari's 1979 play *Christopher Columbus*:

> *Columbus*: The Earth is not flat, Father, it's round!
> *The Prior*: Don't say that!
> *Columbus*: It's the truth; it's not a mill pond strewn
> with islands, it's a sphere.
> *The Prior*: Don't, don't say that; it's blasphemy.[11]

This misrepresentation flattered several American prejudices, but the parallel with other struggles between sweet reason and stubborn revelation did not go unnoticed elsewhere. In France and other continental nations, for example, Columbus, viewed as the bearer of universal enlightenment, was also to find a successful career.

Writing in the 1940s, Samuel Eliot Morison, a canny sailor and generally temperate historian of Columbus, describes Irving's scenes of Columbus in argument with the learned doctors as "pure moonshine" and continues:

> Washington Irving, scenting his opportunity for a picturesque and moving scene, took a fictitious account of this nonexistent university council published 130 years after the event, elaborated on it, and let his imagination go completely. . . . [This] has become one of the most popular Columbus myths; for we all love to hear of professors and experts being confounded by common sense. . . . The whole story is misleading and mischievous nonsense. . . . The sphericity of the globe was not in

14

question. The issue was the width of the ocean; and therein the opposition was right.[12]

Other Political Uses

After 1870 the Flat Error was found to have a second use, this time among what might be called the anti-anti-Darwinists. Darwin's defenders were looking for any ammunition they could muster in their struggle with fundamentalist Christians. None of the major Church Fathers or medieval thinkers would have dreamt of relying solely on the Bible as a guide to scientific matters. Biblical hermeneutics were generally too sophisticated for that. But feeling threatened by some scientific advances, groups of modern Christians tried that desperate tactic. Their zealous over-simplifications gave Darwin's supporters—who were not very theologically sophisticated themselves—a powerful weapon with which to make all so-called "biblical" thought appear benighted.

Dug up by some scholar or other involved in these controversies, the long-forgotten and always negligible Cosmas Indicopleustes was translated into English for the first time in 1897 and was immediately portrayed, not only as a fool himself, but as the emblem of Christian foolishness. His name began to appear in histories and textbooks as if he had been the main cosmological theorist of the Middle Ages. The medieval Church had been a sponsor of science and learning, of course, with figures like Roger Bacon and Albertus Magnus. But this truth was lost as the dynamics of the Darwin controversy were projected back upon the earlier age.

And the transgressors were not only ignorant bigots. Andrew Dickson White, the founder of Cornell University, for example, became one of the principal late-nineteenth-century propagators of the Flat Error out of opposition to contemporary Christian obscurantists. Ignoring the medieval scholarship that was available even in his day, he accepted on faith the misstatements of several fellow polemicists. Russell comments: "White and his colleagues ended by doing what they accused the fathers of, namely, creating

15

a body of false knowledge by consulting one another instead of the evidence."[13]

Though for at least the last fifty years all this has been known to scholars as a simple comedy of errors, the myth persists. Not only does the Flat Error continue to appear in widely used primary, secondary, and college textbooks, it even continues to have pernicious effects on some of the most influential modern histories. The distinguished historian and former Librarian of Congress Daniel Boorstin in his lively and generally reliable volume *The Discoverers*, for example, has been taken in to a degree. In chapters entitled "The Prison of Christian Dogma" and "A Flat Earth Returns," Boorstin asserts that during the Middle Ages Christians engaged in an "amnesiac effort to ignore the growing mass of knowledge [about a spherical earth] and retreat into a world of faith and caricature." As evidence, he cites the hapless and then-still-unknown Cosmas and, in the course of several pages, mixes that eccentric figure with more mainstream Christian thinkers like Augustine to evoke a wholly imaginary "legion of Christian geographers" who believed that the earth was flat.[14]

Boorstin does not go on to make the further vulgar error that Columbus proved the world was round. Somewhat inconsistently, he admits that the experts had turned Columbus down "probably because they thought he had grossly underestimated the sea distance westward to the Indies."[15] Yet coming after the extensive misrepresentation of the state of geographical knowledge in Columbus's time, this brief concession has doubtless done little to prevent the survival of several nineteenth-century myths about Columbus in twentieth-century textbooks and popular lore. Cole Porter's song "They All Laughed" merely records the belief most people held in the earlier part of the twentieth century—and may still hold.

Twentieth-Century Myths

The tenacity of the progressive-Columbus myths that were gathering force in 1892 and beyond should alert us to the possibil-

16

ity that new, unconscious distortions—this time of a very different character—may have colored current versions of the story. For most public commentators now, Columbus is no longer viewed as a proto-progressive. On the contrary, for a spectrum of scholars and activists, he has become the symbolic bearer, not, as his name Christopher signified, of Christ to new lands—except in the sinister sense of destroying native spirituality and culture—but of every evil that Western individualism, capitalism, industrialism, colonialism, and cultural "Eurocentrism" have visited on any part of the world in the last five hundred years.

Every schoolchild used to be taught that Christopher Columbus, a Genoese navigator, discovered America in 1492. But for several years now, a chorus of voices (growing larger and louder as we approached 1992) has assaulted every certainty, except the date, about the Columbus story. Some want to de-emphasize Columbus's significance preemptively by establishing that the Vikings, West Africans, or Asians were here first, though if they were, they left few signs and almost no written records. Others would like to convince us that Columbus or Colón or Colombo or whatever his name may have been in fact was—take your pick —Spanish or Portuguese, Greek or Jewish. Far from being a navigator, moreover, he had never commanded a ship "larger than a rowboat" before setting sail for the New World.[16] Still others, by far the most numerous and ideologically strident, wish to monopolize public attention with claims that Columbus's "discovery" of America is, in any case, nothing to celebrate.

The very term discovery has been ruled out of the official proceedings by some of the principal participants. When Spain first began planning for the commemoration of its role in the New World, it tried to defuse hostile reactions from Native Americans and others who regard the very idea of the discovery of America as evidence of continuing cultural imperialism. Native populations, in this view, did not need to be discovered. They knew who and where they were when the Spaniards arrived. Needing a more neutral term, therefore, Spain and its New World collaborators

17

(primarily Mexico) scoured the softer side of contemporary culture and hit upon *El Encuentro*, "The Encounter of Two Worlds."

The Smithsonian Institution in Washington, D.C., followed suit. Its major quincentenary exhibition, "Seeds of Change," argues that even to speak of Old World and New World is to get the picture wrong. In the words of Herman J. Viola, director of the quincentenary programs at the Museum of Natural History, Columbus's voyage created "one new world from two old worlds."[17] This formula, too, seemed to skirt claims of precedence and superiority.

In itself, seeing 1492 as the meeting of two different cultures has historical value. At the very least, it points to something in what William Carlos Williams once called "The American Grain" that is often overlooked: the continuing presence of native cultures in our world, particularly in certain parts of Latin America. But some native spokesmen refused to accept such compromises. For example, the South and Meso-American Indian Information Center (SAIIC) in Berkeley, California, a self-described liaison between Indian peoples of the North and of the South, and between Indians and non-Indians, issued "A Call to Action!" in 1991 that included the following:

> We ask the Spanish government, the Vatican, and all Latin American and European governments who are promoting the Quincentennial Jubilee, how the steam-rolling of cultures for the enrichment of a European minority can be considered an "Encounter of Two Worlds." . . . The myths about Columbus and the "encounter" are a completely false manipulation of history.[18]

Sympathetic persons are requested to send contributions to the SAIIC offices to help spread the word about the most evident consequences of Columbus's invasion:

> genocide, torture, political, ideological and cultural submission and death through diseases brought to the continent. Our land and our resources have been and continue to be plundered.

Military, ideologic, economic and religious power are the instruments of domination in this conquest.

The Battle Lines

As this excerpt graphically shows, what began as a seemingly just attempt to make appreciation of the two cultures more equal in the Columbus commemoration has quickly shifted into an acrimonious battle to make the non-European side a moralistic stick with which to beat European societies, including their political and cultural heirs in the Americas. Many of the more radical critics of those societies—environmentalists, feminists, African-American organizations, multiculturalist advocates—have vigorously entered the Columbus controversy. Scenting political opportunity, Fidel Castro, one of the last Communist dictators, has declared himself an honorary Native American and denounced Columbus. (When Arthur M. Schlesinger, Jr., slyly pointed out to him during a 1992 visit to Havana that "if it weren't for Columbus, you wouldn't be here," Castro conceded, "Well, Columbus brought good things as well as bad."[19]) Though generalization about such a diverse group is difficult, it is probably fair to say that something like their common view was expressed by Russell Means, one of the leaders of the American Indian Movement: "Columbus makes Hitler look like a juvenile delinquent."[20] Means went on to say that asking Native Americans to celebrate on October 12 is like asking Jews to appreciate a "balanced view of the Holocaust" on Hitler Day.

Few major institutions are willing to defend themselves against this sort of moral and political onslaught. Most have simply sought to avoid confrontation by side-stepping the Columbus issue. In Washington, D.C., the exhibition at the Museum of Natural History, which documented the exchanges of food, plants, and animals after 1492, basically did not address Columbus at all. Neither did Washington's other main museum show that had been prompted by reflections on 1492. The National Gallery of Art displayed objects assembled from several cultures flourish-

19

ing "Circa 1492," and the gallery's director, J. Carter Brown, stressed in the catalogue: "This show is not about a man called Christopher Columbus; his name does not even appear in the title."[21] Instead of examining the record, good and bad, of the man whose efforts make 1992 a significant date, many institutions have, on the contrary, chimed in with support for the breathtaking range of the indictments against him.

Even the churches, which in some sense should be willing to defend their bringing of the good news to new peoples, cannot seem to find any value in the spread of Christianity to the Americas. The U.S. National Council of Churches (NCC), an umbrella Protestant organization that for years has advocated progressive causes, seems to see in the European arrival not a badly flawed social integration, at least partly redeemed by evangelization, but genocide *tout court*—several interlocking genocides and rapes, in fact, of the land, of peoples, and of raw materials. In the brief statement on the quincentenary that the NCC issued in 1990, genocide was mentioned several times per page, while evangelization, in a positive sense, was not mentioned at all.[22] For the NCC, evangelization was solely a pretext for exploitation; the quincentenary, then, should be an occasion not for rejoicing but for repentance.

In fact, only the U.S. Catholic bishops and their Latin American counterparts, along with a few prelates in Spain and Rome, have been willing to praise the evangelization, though they admit it was marred by profoundly un-Christian acts.[23] Yet many Catholics too have taken up the radical critique. Liberation theologians in Latin America seem to have replaced now moribund Marxism with anti-1492 thought. One U.S. Catholic bishop, part Native American himself, has even called on the Knights of Columbus to change their name.[24] For many of the religious critics, genocide and rape of women, of the land, and of culture stand at the dark heart of all non-indigenous American societies and cultures, north and south.

20

The Indictment

Native American and African-American self-assertion in 1992 is as understandable as Irish Catholic and Italian-American self-assertion was in 1892. Both anniversaries allow some forgotten truths to be told, whatever distortions may simultaneously be introduced. But a much larger storm has also been brewing—what can only be described as a historical indictment of Columbus and European imperialism, as well as of European culture and all its works and pomps. These charges are aided by sympathy for some groups that were subjected to very real and almost unprecedented evils during the age of discovery. Columbus In Context, an activist militant group founded in New York in 1990, described the quincentenary as the best political opportunity for progressives "since the Vietnam War"[25] and issued a statement calling for the rejection of the mariner as a national hero: "He organized an extermination of native Americans. He was also mean, cruel and greedy in small matters as he was in vast ones." Hans Koning, a novelist and long-time opponent of Columbus who is the apparent author of this statement, argues that we must open our eyes to the past:

> We must end the phoney baloney about the white man bringing Christianity, and about Columbus the noble son of the humble weaver. Our false heroes and a false sense of the meaning of courage and manliness have too long burdened our national spirit.[26]

The radical critique clearly indicts the United States in general as much as it does Columbus.

Perhaps the most powerful formulation of this indictment to appear as 1992 approached, however, was Kirkpatrick Sale's revisionist biography *The Conquest of Paradise: Christopher Columbus and the Columbian Legacy*. Significantly, Sale is not a professional historian but a political and environmental activist, a co-director of the E. F. Schumacher Society, and a founder of the New York

21

Green Party. Sale's reading of Columbus's legacy had considerable impact on sympathetic teachers, journalists, and the general public because of both its stylistic and analytical brilliance and its widespread distribution as a main selection of the Book-of-the-Month Club.

Many newly emphasized truths about Columbus the man, his voyages, and his legacy are disturbing. Here was a daring sailor, a visionary who brought the Americas and Europe together, but also a man with many human flaws, the product in part of a culture in turmoil. His story is both epic and tragic in that his monumental achievement is intertwined with the high and low human qualities closely related in him. Kirkpatrick Sale believes, along with many others since Francisco López de Gómara first said it, that Columbus is "the most important figure in human history," but in a negative sense.[27] His account of 1492 and after is a relentless venting of bile. Sale is vivid, learned, obsessed, sneering, contemptuous, skeptical of anything that reflects well on Columbus or European culture, and ultimately credulous about every evil attributed or attributable to Columbus, by himself or others. In addition he presents with renewed contemporary credulity the old myth of noble savages and ignoble Europeans.

Noble and Ignoble Savages

The opposition of noble savages (NSS) to savage Western civilization (SWC) is by now a commonplace of our culture. First introduced by Montesquieu and later perfected by Rousseau about two-and-a-half centuries ago, this theme has been transposed since into several different keys pitting East Indians, black Africans, Communist Chinese, revolutionary Cubans, Sandinista Nicaraguans, and Native Americans against evil Western counterparts. But Kirkpatrick Sale achieves a new high-water mark in the purity of his NSS and the utter blackness of his SWC.

If this seems an exaggeration, witness the following passage in which we are informed that not only did the NSS at the time of Columbus's landing live in social harmony amidst natural abun-

22

dance of food and other needs. They lived, it appears, in a kind of prelapsarian garden where disease itself was virtually unknown:

> One reason that the Indian populations, in the Caribbean as elsewhere, were so vulnerable to diseases of any kind is that, to an extraordinary extent, the Americas were free of any serious pathogens. The presumed passage of the original populations across the Bering Strait tens of thousands of years before served to freeze to death most human disease carriers except a few intestinal ones, it is thought, and there were apparently none established on the continents previously, so in general the Indians enjoyed remarkably good health, free of both endemic and epidemic scourges. As Henry Dobyns says in his examination of aboriginal North American populations, *Their Number Become Thinned*, "People simply did not very often die of illnesses" before the Europeans came.[28]

Importantly, the argument here is not that indigenous Americans were susceptible to European diseases because they had never before encountered them; rather, they were free of serious disease in general. They lived in a kind of medical paradise.

At times Sale seems to be suggesting that, if only we were willing to fly over to eastern Siberia and make the trip *al fresco* again while the continent was being fumigated, we might return to this blissful state. There is little chance of our doing so, however, because, as Sale portrays us, we are all descendants of late-medieval European culture, which he characterizes as a culture of death. Some innocents may think of the early sixteenth century as the time of Reformation and Counter-Reformation, Renaissance progress, and a march toward a fuller humanism, but Sale will allow none of this. Where we may see complexity or ambiguity, Sale sees an evil monolith that has survived basically unchanged through the intervening centuries, "a Europe that in thought and deed was estranged from its natural environment and had for several thousand years [!] been engaged in depleting and destroying the land and waters it depended on, and justifying that with one or another creed or conviction."[29] Though Sale lays much of the blame for Western ecocide on biblical impulses, he shows a

23

kind of evenhandedness here: he is willing to concede that Western civilization was deeply ill even before the advent of such anti-natural spiritual movements. Classical scholars will be interested to learn that the Roman Empire fell because its exploitation of nature had led to "its own inability to feed itself."[30]

For Sale, Europe's divorcing of itself from nature made it rootless and restless, sick and unstable, powerful but hollow. Late-medieval Europe, he argues (mostly by selective quotation from other historians), exhibited these characteristics in a uniquely strong form. And he sees in Columbus the very incarnation of all these negative qualities. Sale's Columbus is not a daring seaman with a vision of something of which even the navigator himself was not fully conscious. Instead, this Columbus is a man without family or community ties, ready to sail anywhere because nothing constrained him or moved him to loyalty. His motives, insofar as identifiable motives drive such a deeply disturbed man, centered around early capitalist greed and early Renaissance ambition for power and status. Any doubts about this interpretation can be laid to rest by reading Columbus's *Journal* of the first voyage. There, according to Sale, the impulse toward exploitation of nature and the lust for gold dominate, and the meager descriptions of the flora and fauna of the New World make it clear that Columbus has no idea of—let alone any interest in—what he is looking at.

Neither did the Europe of Columbus's time react to the discovery, in Sale's view, with the proper curiosity and wonder: "Certainly there was no intellectual explosion, nothing that 'caused Europe to realize that the perimeters of their world were changing' and 'to reevaluate their concept of the world' (as a recent study has put it)."[31] The Europeans, insofar as they looked up from their constant preoccupation with evil deeds and death, merely saw the new lands as wealth to be exploited. The right to colonization was assumed by Christian intruders who missed

an opportunity for a dispirited and melancholy Europe to have learned something about fecundity and regeneration, about social comeliness and amity, about harmony with the natural

24

world. The appropriate architecture for Colón to have envisioned along these shores might have been a forum, or an amphitheater, or an academy, perhaps an auditorium or a tabernacle; instead, a fortress.[32]

During his lifetime Columbus used to get gratuitous advice from people in "safe berths there in Spain." Writing from the relative security of the Empire State, Kirkpatrick Sale joins that line of long-distance critics.

The lessons Sale draws from the Columbus story are perhaps the most telling aspect of his study:

> There is only one way to live in America, and there can be only one way, and that is as Americans—the original Americans—for that is what the earth of America demands. We have tried for five centuries to resist that simple truth. We resist it further only at the risk of the imperilment—worse, the likely destruction—of the earth.[33]

Sale ridicules Columbus, the medieval dreamer, for thinking he was near the earthly paradise when he discovered four rivers running together in a beautiful region of what is now Venezuela, a scene that reminded him of the description in the book of Genesis. Yet biblical myths are powerful. Sale titles his book the *Conquest of Paradise*, and predicts something very like the Last Judgment if we do not repent of our Western ways. Native American ways mirrored a perfect life in the Garden of Eden and point the way toward the New Jerusalem. Claims of that magnitude are not uncommon in the new Columbus literature.

New Age and New World

As unlikely a candidate as Christopher Columbus may appear for pure angel or pure devil, his exploits have been drawn into the larger debate now going on about the nature of American culture. Just as in 1892 confident, progressive Americans identified with a confident, progressive explorer, so in 1992 troubled, pessimistic Americans see in Columbus an image of everything wrong with contemporary American life. A 1992 PBS television series on primitive peoples went so far as to accuse Columbus of exporting consumerism to the New World, though consumerism does not seem to have been exactly rampant in medieval Spain.[34] On the face of it, five hundred years of evil seem a lot to attribute to the influence of one man. Logically, if Columbus is to receive all the blame by virtue of a massive *post hoc ergo propter hoc,* then he should also receive all the credit for whatever good has occurred in those five hundred years. Yet it is far more common in 1992 to criticize him for the legacy of slavery, conquest, and imperialism, as well as for the cultural arrogance, male domination, militarism, and environmental insensitivities alleged to make up the core of modern American life.

The old heroic view of Columbus was a myth. But is the new view of this sailor from Genoa the needed corrective to former idealistic portraits? Is Columbus as black, and his legacy as unrelievedly evil, as the radical critics claim? Or is Harvard historian Stephen Thernstrom right when he says that Kirkpatrick Sale "tells the tale with about as much balance and judiciousness as we might expect in a history of the United States written in the Soviet Union in the darkest days of Stalin's rule."[35] Older biographers of Columbus like Samuel Eliot Morison were not unaware of some bad precedents set by Columbus. Yet anything less than a sweeping denunciation of five hundred years of Western history—that is, anything less than lining up behind views like those of Sale— is now regarded by many people as a simple continuation of imperialism.

The following chapters examine several of the particulars in the indictment of Columbus. Hans Koning and Columbus In Context are partly right: we need to know the full truth about the American past, even when it cuts across present pieties of whatever stripe. Popular accounts of American history *have* been too uniformly rosy, obscuring the fact that the United States has been and is made up of a group of imperfect human beings with a mixed history, a foul rag-and-bone shop like all human societies. Knowing the full truth about our past—even the unsavory parts—need not weaken us. Rather, it should make us both more modest about our expectations and prouder of the true achievements that have taken place on these shores in the past five hundred years.

But we also need the truth to prevent a further imperialistic imposition on the very peoples the radical critics wish to defend. Some parts of Native American cultures were admirable and deserve preservation. Others decidedly were not, as shall be shown in some detail in the following pages. Using Native American culture as a pawn in contemporary political debates only serves to damage, once more, the true record of what they achieved—and did not achieve. It is no favor to Native Americans or African-Americans today to redefine their heritage to suit, yet again, the needs of white culture.

Carrying out these two investigations requires serious work, not facile assumptions. Contemporary scholars frequently invoke the question of "the other"—a useful notion so long as we remember that it is always difficult to know the other, particularly when that other lived in a different culture several centuries ago. This sense of the difficulty in knowing the other, however, is rarely evident even in university environments. In early 1992, for example, the student senate at the University of Cincinnati voted to declare a "Columbus-myth-free Campus,"[36] giving voice to a sentiment probably well represented on many campuses in the 1990s. But that goal is far more demanding than the students suppose. It is highly doubtful that any of them—perhaps even any of the adults advising them—have much acquaintance with the myths, facts, lacunae, and legitimate difficulties in interpretation about Columbus. Two of the soundest recent biographers of Columbus have observed that, along with its other educational failures, "the United States seems to have lost, rather than gained, knowledge about Columbus since 1892. Most people reach adulthood with only the most rudimentary knowledge about him, half-remembered from a few lessons in elementary school."[37] Arriving at truth, college students were once taught, takes intellectual

27

effort; repeating ideas that happen to be in the air takes none. Without careful study the impulse to cast aside other people's myths for what we think are obvious truths creates myths of its own.

2

El Almirante

Let us hear what their comments are now—those who are
so ready with accusations and quick to find fault, saying
from their safe berths there in Spain, "Why didn't you do
this or that when you were over there." I'd like to see their
sort on this adventure. Verily I believe, there's another
journey, of quite a different order, for them to make, or all
our faith is vain.

—Columbus
Lettera Rarissima[1]

After centuries of controversies, the life of Columbus lies beneath mountains of interpretation and misinterpretation.
Sharp criticism of *El Almirante* (the admiral)—and sharp reaction
to it—go back to the very beginnings of his explorations, as the
passage cited above, written at a particularly threatening moment
during Columbus's fourth and final voyage to the New World,
graphically shows. Then, as now, it was easy for people who had
never dared comparable feats to suggest how the whole business
might have been done better. And in truth, Columbus's manifest
errors and downright incapacities as a leader of men, anywhere
but on the sea, played into the hands of his critics and properly
made him the target of protests. His failures in leadership provoked atrocities against the Caribbean natives and harsh punishment, including executions, of Spaniards as well. Stubbornness,
obsessiveness, and paranoia often dominated his psyche. Even
many of his closest allies in the initial ventures clashed with him

29

over one thing or another. In the wake of the titanic passions his epochal voyages unleashed, it is no wonder that almost every individual and event connected with his story has been praised or damned by someone during the past five hundred years.

Elusive Facts

Attempts to account for the various and apparently contradictory things Columbus said and did have raised doubts about even the most basic facts of his personal history. In spite of all the quincentennial scholarly ferment, however, many traditional teachings about Columbus's early life remain the most probable explanations for the data we have. Born in Genoa, like Venice one of the most important Mediterranean trading powers of the time, he sailed early to lands as distant as the Greek island of Chios and Ireland, perhaps even Iceland. He plied the Atlantic seaboard from England to the coast of Guinea in Africa. Eventually, most likely in the 1480s, he settled in Portugal, became a chart-maker, and married a Portuguese wife of the lesser nobility. Sometime during these years, he conceived the idea of sailing west to the Indies and petitioned the Portuguese king for financial support and state sponsorship before turning to Spain.

But much of this is plausible conjecture. In the introduction to the Columbus documents published by the Hakluyt Society in 1929 and 1932, Cecil Jane remarked that evidence available for determining the early practical experience and beliefs of Columbus is scanty and unsatisfactory: "In such circumstances, dogmatism on the question would be entirely misplaced. To assert that, before he had discovered the New World, Columbus held any given opinion would be to assert something wholly impossible of proof."[2] New evidence has surfaced since then that clears up beyond reasonable doubt certain problems. Oxford historian Felipe Fernández-Armesto has reviewed the current state of scholarly knowledge and opinion in his 1991 biography *Columbus*, the most sober, penetrating, and least partisan of the crop of quincentenary books.[3] But Jane's warning should still be heeded. The primary

30

material about Columbus leaves many issues unresolved, and perhaps unresolvable.

Anyone approaching this material for the first time should be especially cautions. Numerous theories have been proposed to fill in gaps and reconcile contradictions, including various solutions to alleged mysteries about Columbus the man and his intentions. Denigrators of Columbus generally believe that the gaps exist because he was not considered very important at the time of his death. But this is to project scholarly frustrations back on a rather full record. Though Columbus's fortunes had certainly declined toward the end of his life and made the records of his final years less detailed than we might wish, the amount of biographical data concerning him is relatively large compared to that concerning his near contemporaries. John Cabot, for example, who "discovered" North America for the British, was also probably Genoese (Giovanni Cabotto) and was born roughly the same time as Columbus. Yet no immediate written records of his voyages, or much about the man, have come down to us. Everything is second or thirdhand save a few documents placing him in Venice (if this is the same Cabot) and England.[4] Measured against the paucity of information about Cabot and other explorers of the Americas, Columbus's dossier is quite thick.

Through a Glass Darkly

But the wealth of material is deceptive. The several surviving letters, memoranda, wills, and annotations in books—all written by the admiral himself—do not yield an unambiguous portrait. Furthermore, two of the earliest secondary sources, Fernando Columbus's life of his father and Bartolomé de Las Casas's *History of the Indies*, are marked by partisan passions. Fernando clearly wishes to portray the admiral as a great, pious, and noble man hounded by fools and evildoers—as a grand figure whose claims on revenues from the New World for himself and his descendants should be honored by the Spanish monarchs in perpetuity. For Las Casas, a Dominican priest who became famous as the foremost defender of the Indians, Columbus evokes mixed emotions. He is a great hero whom Las Casas saw make his triumphal return to Seville on Palm Sunday 1493 after the first voyage but also, inadvertently, a villain.

Writing decades after 1492 with a fervor bordering on fanaticism, Las Casas's main intentions are to denounce mistreatment of the natives and to convince the Spanish crown to stop it. While he holds Columbus, whom he knew personally, in high esteem, he also blames him for beginning that mistreatment, which he paints in lurid detail. Las Casas underplays or ignores more amicable relations between Spaniards and natives. His book *The Very Brief Relation*, as many scholars have noted, gave Spain's sixteenth-century enemies—a large group of nations consisting of political competitors and emerging Protestant powers—the data with which to concoct the *leyenda negra* (black legend) of the Spanish Empire. Ironically, Spain's very openness to publishing and debating its actions in the New World made it appear far worse than countries like England and the Netherlands, which also committed atrocities but without the negative publicity.

Las Casas is also our source—thirdhand—for one of the most crucial records, Columbus's *Log* of the first voyage. We know that scribes reproduced the original manuscript in two fair copies. One, presented to Queen Isabella, was eventually lost. The other was lost as well after Las Casas had made extensive extracts and paraphrases from it for his history. Scholars have reconstructed this *Log* from passages in Las Casas, but given the intervening hands and Las Casas's two powerful passions, love of Columbus and horror at the mistreatment of natives, we can only speculate on what distortions have been introduced into the text.

Fact and Imagination

The temptation to project modern categories back upon earlier historical periods is always strong. Reviewing these first late-fifteenth-century contacts now, with knowledge of what befell indigenous peoples later, we are particularly inclined to read large-scale portents into small events. If Columbus mentions how easy it would be to subdue the natives, or expresses impatience with his failure to find the high and rich civilization of Asia, many historians readily fall into the error of seeing his attitudes as a combination of careless imperialism and greed, or even as a symbol of all that was to follow. We would do well to recall, however, that the Spanish record after Columbus is complex and not wholly bad, particularly in its gradual elaboration of native rights (see chapter three).

In Columbus the man, several conflicting currents existed side by side. Las Casas is an important witness here because of both his passionate commitment to justice for Indians and his personal association with Columbus for several years. In a telling remark, Las Casas notes that while Christopher's brother, Bartolomé, was a resolute leader, he lacked the "sweetness and benignity" of the admiral.[5] Columbus's noble bearing and gentle manners are confirmed in many other sources. Nevertheless, Las Casas can be harsh in his criticism. Chapter 119 of *History of the Indies* concludes with the judgment that both brothers mistakenly began to occupy land and exact tribute owing to "the most culpable ignorance, which has no excuse, of natural and divine law."[6]

After five hundred years it may seem impossible to reconcile the contradictory traits Las Casas mentions. He attempted an explanation of his own:

Truly, I would not dare blame the admiral's intentions, for I knew him well and I know his intentions were good. But . . . the road he paved and the things he did of his own free will, as well as sometimes under constraint, stemmed from his ignorance of the law. There is much to ponder here and one can see the guiding principle of this whole Indian enterprise, namely, as is clear from the previous chapters, that the admiral and his Christians, as well as all those who followed after him in this land, worked on the assumption that the way to achieve their desires was first and foremost to instill fear in these people, to the extent of making the name Christian synonymous with terror. And to do this, they performed outstanding feats never

33

before invented or dreamed of, as, God willing, I will show later. And this is contrary and inimical to the way that those who profess Christian benignity, gentleness and peace ought to negotiate the conversion of infidels.[7]

As this excerpt shows, Las Casas's style of writing and mode of reasoning do not always yield great clarity, and his assessment here begs several questions. Columbus's policies, and official Spanish policy generally, were much more given to gentleness and kindness in the beginning than Las Casas, who only witnessed later troubled times, allows to appear. There is no question that conflicts with natives and factional infighting among Spaniards drove the admiral to more onerous measures, including enslavement of Indians captured in military actions.

While Las Casas's condemnation is cast in terms of absolute justice and as such has permanent relevance to evaluating Columbus's role in the New World, we should remember that Columbus was placed in unprecedented circumstances and should not be judged in the same way as we would a modern trained anthropologist. Paolo Emilio Taviani, an admiring but not uncritical recent biographer of Columbus, demonstrates the difficulty attending every particular of the first contact:

The European scale of values was different from that of the natives. "They give everything for a trifle"; obviously what was a trifle on the European scale was not so for the natives. For them "a potsherd or a broken glass cup" was worth "sixteen skeins of cotton." Columbus warned that would never do, because from unrestricted trade between the two mentalities, the two conceptions of value, grave injustices would result, and so he immediately prohibited the cotton trade, allowing no one to take any and reserving the acquisition entirely for the king of Spain. A just prohibition, not easy to impose on ninety men —what strength could it have when nine hundred, nine thousand, or ninety thousand Europeans would arrive? Such were the first troubles in an encounter between two worlds that did not understand one another.[8]

If we wish to task Columbus for all the asymmetries that ensued, we should credit him as well for this initial attempt, later repeated by many Spanish governors and theologians, to find some just route through the thicket of massive cultural difference. He failed and permitted far more wicked practices than unequal trade, but we should not let subsequent events blind us to his authentic concern for justice in the first contacts.

Some Brighter Moments

In spite of the cultural gulf, mutual affections and understanding did, at times, appear. After over two months of exploration in the Caribbean, Columbus's ship, the *Santa Maria*, went aground on Christmas 1492 in what is now Haiti. There Columbus encountered a people and a chief so helpful that his log entries for the following days view the entire episode as providential. He would never have chosen, as he admits, to come ashore or build the settlement of La Navidad (Christmas) there. He did not like the harbor at all. Yet he concluded that his relations with the Taínos and their chief Guacanagarí must be part of a divine plan in light of the friendship that sprung up between the two peoples.

Some Columbus scholars, perhaps a bit jaded from staring overlong at the historical lacunae and inconsistencies of the man, see in these log entries only an attempt to cover up the disastrous loss of the ship or a propaganda ploy to make the Spanish monarchs think well of the discoveries. Robert H. Fuson, a modern translator of the log, is a marine historian rather than a Columbus specialist. He is sometimes rightly criticized for his rather naive historical interpretations.[9] But it is precisely because he is not predisposed to suspicion that he notices something overlooked by scholars occupied with weighing too many contradictory theories about the Haiti episode:

> Affection for the young chief in Haiti, and vice versa, is one of the most touching stories of love, trust, and understanding between men of different races and cultures to come out of this period in history. His [Columbus's] instructions to the men he left behind at La Navidad, for January 2, clearly illustrate his sincere fondness and respect for the Indians.[10]

The January 2 entry, as we shall see below, indicates that Columbus had some ulterior motives in placating the natives. But that does not negate his genuine good feeling toward them or his gratitude for their generosity. Even if we assume that Columbus is putting the best interpretation on events for Ferdinand and Isabella, some sort of fellow feeling undeniably had arisen, at least temporarily, across the vast cultural divide separating the Taínos and the Europeans. Despite the great evils that would come later, this altruism was not without its own modest legacies.

An extreme but common form of the over-simple charges often leveled against the Europeans in general and Columbus in particular has come from the pen of the novelist Hans Koning. Writing in the *Washington Post* to influence public sentiments about the quincentenary, Koning insisted that from 1492 to 1500,

> there is not one recorded moment of awe, of joy, of love, of a smile. There is only anger, cruelty, greed, terror, and death. That is the record. Nothing else, I hold, is relevant when we discuss our commemoration of its 500th anniversary.[11]

Riding the wave of revisionism about American history now sweeping over education, Koning made these claims under the title "Teach the Truth About Columbus."

The only problem with his assessment is that every particular in his catalog of what constitutes the truth is false. To take them in order: Columbus certainly records awe at his discoveries throughout his four voyages. His praise of the land's beauty was partly meant, of course, to convince the king and queen of the value of the properties Columbus had discovered for them. But some of it is simply awe; Columbus's enthusiasm for many of the new lands reaches a climax when he describes the sheer loveliness of the Venezuelan coast, which he believed to be the site of the original Garden of Eden, the earthly paradise. If that is not a record of awe, it is difficult to imagine what would be.

The relations between natives and Spaniards before 1500 are not, *pace* Koning, unrelieved darkness either. If anything, they are

36

a frustrating reminder of a road not taken. Smiles there were—
recorded smiles—at least on the native Taíno side: "They love
their neighbors as themselves, and they have the softest and
gentlest voices in the world and are always smiling" (*Log*, Tuesday,
25 December 1492). Columbus had reason to appreciate these
people since they had just helped him salvage what was salvageable
from the wreck of the *Santa Maria*. In the feast natives and
Spaniards held after the rescue, the cacique Guacanagarí placed a
crown on Columbus's head. The admiral reciprocated by giving
him a scarlet cloak and a pair of colored boots, "and I placed upon
his finger a large silver ring. I had been told that he had seen a
silver ring on one of my sailors and desired it very much. The
King was joyful and overwhelmed." Guacanagarí grew so close to
Columbus that he asked if he and his brother might return with
him to Castile.[12]

When it came time to leave for Spain, Columbus placed thirty-
nine men "under the command of three officers, all of whom are
very friendly to King Guacanagarí," and furthermore ordered that
"they should avoid *as they would death* annoying or tormenting the
Indians, bearing in mind how much they owe these people." The
emphasis added to this last quotation has a double purpose.
Clearly, Columbus recognized the temptations his men would
have; just as clearly he was determined, to the best of his ability,
to anticipate and block those temptations. This is the entry of
January 2 that Fuson reads as expressing sincere kindness and
affection. That reading may be a little too simple, but it is not
entirely mistaken.

What this incident and the founding of the settlement definitely
are *not*, however, are instances of simple European arrogance and ·
imperialism, or what John Noble Wilford, a recent biographer of
Columbus, has called "a personal transition from discoverer to
imperialist."[13] Even when full-scale war between some Indians
and Spaniards broke out during Columbus's second voyage, Guacanagarí remained loyal to Columbus in spite of—or perhaps in
opposition to—commands from another local chief, Caonabó,
for a cacique alliance. No source denies this loyalty between the

Taíno and the admiral, even under trying cultural tensions and warfare. Though we are right to abhor many far-less-happy subsequent events between the inhabitants of the two worlds, the record of the early interaction is richer and more diverse than most people, blinded by contemporary polemics, think. Hans Koning might do well to calm down and read some of these passages.

The List of Charges

The principal moral questions about Columbus arise essentially from three of his actions:

1. He immediately kidnapped some Taínos during his first voyage for questioning and use as interpreters. In that act he showed not only his contempt for Indian life but his belief that Spanish language, culture, and religion were superior and rightly to be imposed on native peoples.

2. After the destruction of La Navidad and the turmoil that ensued during the second voyage, Columbus foolishly ordered exploratory missions without adequate safeguards to restrain outrageously violent men like Mosen Pedro Margarit and Alonso de Ojeda. He then punished the natives who objected to Spaniards living off the land or who resisted their commands. In addition to setting this evil precedent, he shipped home some natives to become slaves with a very poor excuse:

> Since of all the islands those of the cannibals are much the largest and much more fully populated, it is thought here that to take some of the men and women and to send them home to Castile would not be anything but well, for they may one day be led to abandon that inhuman custom that they have of eating men, and there in Castile, learning the language, they will much more readily receive baptism and secure the welfare of their souls.[14]

3. Columbus instituted a system of gold tribute from the natives that was heavy—nearly impossible, in fact, given the small quantity of gold on the island of Hispaniola—and that was harshly enforced.

Each of these charges is true and no amount of admiration for Christopher Columbus can excuse what is simply inexcusable. Even the argument by Felipe Fernández-Armesto, one of the fairest Columbus historians, that "Columbus and his successors were guilty only of applying the best standards of their time" makes two false assumptions.[15] First, that such behavior represents the best contemporary standards. As we shall see in the next chapter, when we examine the religious influences during the exploration, it did not. Second, that individuals should not be criticized for acting like the majority of their contemporaries because they are bound by culture and history. The latter argument draws strength from current philosophical schools that hold there are no privileged or absolute positions outside of historically conditioned views. But if we think we should condemn Aztec human sacrifice as wrong—not simply a different cultural form, but wrong—then we must admit there are universal principles that also allow us to criticize improper European use of force, enslavement, and exploitation.

Yet just as we try to understand the reasons behind Aztec human sacrifice or Carib cannibalism, and both tribes' imperialism toward other native peoples, we should also try to see what led to Columbus's behavior. Columbus, as Las Casas testified above, was not by nature a brutal man like Ojeda or Cortés. The first sign of harshness by him, in fact, seems to have been his acquiescence, during the second voyage, in a death sentence against some Indians on Hispaniola who had been caught stealing. Significantly, the pleading of another Indian moved him to remit the sentence in that case (the wavering too is characteristic of his uncertainty in handling questions of governance). Though he apparently regarded the Indians as inferior and always approached them with much the same assumption of superiority that Spaniards approached the Guanches of the Canary Islands and African tribes, he seemed at least partly—and when circumstances allowed—aware that good treatment was both morally called for and favorable to Spanish interests.

39

A fairer reading of the record reveals some mitigating factors, though these by no means add up to an exoneration.

1. Though Columbus did kidnap some Indians, two interpreters among them, he set one of them free immediately upon returning to Hispaniola during the second voyage.[16] He hoped that the Indian set at liberty would tell others of Spain's wonders and of Columbus's good intentions. This was naive, crude, and manipulative on his part, but shows some perspicacity and good will.

2. Slavery was always a bone of contention between Columbus and the Spanish monarchs—they vehemently opposed this way of "civilizing" their subjects in the Indies. Columbus was not clear in his own mind about the issue. As late as the third voyage, the last in which he would be permitted to visit the growing colony on Hispaniola, Columbus ordered that slaves could only be taken during just war. His thinking was muddled, as was the thinking of the world for at least another half century until several crucial questions about Indian rights and just claims were sorted out (see chapter three).

3. The imposition of gold tribute for Spanish services stemmed from the belief that much gold existed on Hispaniola. And Indian failures to meet what seemed to the Spaniards modest levies were mistakenly attributed to laziness. Indians loved the tiny hawk's bells that the Spaniards brought as trinkets; asking them to fill a bell with gold every two months seemed a reasonable request. Since all governments tax in some fashion, Spain was doing only what caciques and Carib conquerors had been doing for time immemorial. The Spanish system did not "introduce" a new evil to an idyllic people without politics, but it proved peculiarly burdensome because it was imposed from the outside and in ignorance of the realities on Hispaniola. Furthermore, contrary to many wild charges, the Spaniards never intended to commit "genocide." A ready supply of native workers served Spanish self-interest. European and African diseases, however, soon laid waste whole tribes.

Fernández-Armesto argues that Columbus's recourse to violence on Hispaniola resulted mostly from his basic inability to rule well, from "misjudgment rather than wickedness."[17] Gonzalo Fernandez de Oviedo, who became the official Spanish historian of the New World, said that to govern the Hispaniola colony correctly a person would have to be "angelic indeed superhuman."[18] Columbus was far from either; in fact, he was far from possessing even normal political acumen. During his second and third voyages he clearly tried to avoid facing political difficulties on Hispaniola by exploring further.[19] The problem was not merely lack of political skill. As a foreigner, he felt that he could trust only family members and close personal friends. (In fact, recent research has revealed that the Columbus family belonged to an anti-Spanish faction in Genoa, a political embarrassment that may help account for some of Columbus's reticence about his early life.[20]) The resentments arising from difficult conditions, moreover, served to reinforce his tendencies toward paranoia. His rule of both Indians and Spanish oscillated between being too indecisive and too harsh.

We should also understand the kinds of Indians and colonists he had to govern. Columbus had trouble enough with the natives and complained:

> At home they judge me as a governor sent to Sicily or to a city or two under settled government and where the laws can be fully maintained, without fear of all being lost. . . . I ought to be judged as a captain who went from Spain to the Indies to conquer a people, warlike and numerous, and with customs and beliefs very different from ours.[21]

Even the Taínos were probably far less gentle than Columbus earlier reported and "not so innocent as Las Casas tried to show."[22] The Caribs, their fierce, cannibalistic enemies, seem to have been as terrified of the supposedly pacific Taínos as vice versa. And recent archeological investigations suggest that the Taínos, contrary to Columbus's impression of them as being without religion, had a complex system of belief and ritual akin to those in Central America and Mexico. They appear to have played a ritual ball game re-enacting the cosmic struggle between light and

41

darkness and ending with the religious sacrifice of one or more human victims. An early Spanish conquistador estimated that twenty thousand people were sacrificed yearly on Hispaniola alone, though that figure may be wildly exaggerated.[23] In any event, native tribes were profoundly *other* to the unsophisticated sailors and explorers in Columbus's day—and remain profoundly other to us today.

The Spaniards with whom Columbus had to deal were not much better. After the second voyage he asked the monarchs to think carefully about whom they were sending on the voyages and to choose "such persons that there be no suspicion of them and that they consider the purpose for which they have been sent rather than their personal interests."[24] Not only were some of the colonists unusually violent, but many Spanish gentlemen who had come expecting easy wealth resented Columbus, the need to work, and the unhealthy conditions on the island. In dealing with these settlers, as Las Casas observed, "The Admiral had to use violence, threats, and constraint to have the work done at all."[25]

Nicolás de Ovando, an experienced and talented leader appointed later by Spain to rule Hispaniola, also had difficulties in establishing order, but he succeeded in a relatively short time. Columbus did not possess Ovando's gifts. Given all the adverse circumstances, it is not surprising that Columbus himself ended up in chains at the end of the third voyage. Complaints about his governance prompted Ferdinand and Isabella to send Francisco de Bobadilla to help administer the colony. When Bobadilla disembarked, he found five Spaniards hanging from the gallows; they had been executed for crimes by Columbus's orders. Seven more Spaniards were scheduled for the same punishment. In the widespread turmoil Bobadilla decided to arrest the admiral, put him in chains, and ship him back to Spain in 1500. Columbus was forbidden afterward to visit Hispaniola. Officials there were so determined to keep him from exerting any further influence on the island that they would not let him come ashore even during a bad storm while he lay at anchor outside the harbor on the fourth voyage.

Modern Eclipse

In our time a basic skepticism toward heroes, a general guilt over colonialism, and a profound alienation from contemporary culture have led some writers to overemphasize the less savory side of the Columbus story. Sometimes, as in Koning, that perspective eclipses everything else. The desire to correct an idealized image of Columbus tempts us into new falsehoods and blind spots. For that very reason the record has to be examined carefully. A useful thought experiment is to try to imagine what a historian, looking back at 1992 on the occasion of the sexicentenary, might regard as errors induced by late-twentieth-century biases.

One strong current tendency, for example, is to belittle even the courage and achievement of Columbus in making the first Atlantic crossing. In the twentieth century, long trips are far less daunting and stir people's imaginations far less than at any previous time in human history. We step onto comfortable airliners and arrive within hours at any destination on the globe. Only a few decades ago most people were astonished that a lone man could fly the *Spirit of St. Louis* from New York to Paris. Even ships take only six days to cross the Atlantic today, and they are usually equipped with amenities, safety features, and communications equipment that make them almost as comfortable as a modern city—and given the nature of the modern city, probably less risky to life and limb. Our low opinion of the physical bravery required to make the first Atlantic crossing reflects more our own material advantages than the reality of the deed.

The first European Atlantic crossing (at least the first that we are sure took place) began September 8, 1492, from the Canary Islands on three roughly seventy-foot boats; land was not sighted again until October 12 somewhere in the Caribbean.[26] After months of exploration, the return trip began January 16, 1493, and came to a harrowing end when three days of unusually fierce storms separated the two remaining ships. Columbus limped into the Azores February 17, and then took a couple more weeks to reach Lisbon on March 4. The entire journey had taken almost six months.

But the rigors of that ordeal paled in comparison to those suffered by Columbus and over one hundred explorers while they were marooned on Jamaica during the fourth voyage. The governors on the quickly growing colony of Hispaniola spent a year sorting out political questions before bothering to send a rescue ship. Threatening natives, unfamiliar food, and the Indies' pleasant but different climate made every maneuver difficult. It shows a profound lack of imagination and sympathy to say, as many have, that it was no great feat and someone would have done it sooner or later anyway. Many explorers, even years after 1492, would not return to tell their stories.

Experience, Courage, Knowledge

Columbus's achievement lay not only in his daring; it also lay in his determination to take a risk on the basis of growing knowledge. Columbus was primarily a sailor, but a sailor who read and thought under the influence of a vision. Observation of the winds in the Atlantic convinced him that he might catch westbound winds from the Canaries and east-bound returning winds farther north. In this he was brilliantly right. His study of the Florentine cartographer and mathematician Paolo Toscanelli's work and his careful perusal of various other geographical and travel books made the trip seem possible. Columbus seriously erred here, however. As we saw in chapter one, he grossly underestimated the distance west across the Atlantic from Europe to Japan (an error he shared with his contemporary Martin Behaim, who constructed one of the first modern globes).[27] But he was lucky in that Cuba is located almost exactly where he thought Japan should be.

Probably no one until that first New World voyage had deliberately, and successfully, spent so much time sailing out of sight of land as had Columbus. The Portuguese who started working their way down the West African coast in the fifteenth century and the

Chinese who began exploring the Indian Ocean at about the same time both engaged in some brave seamanship. But the Portuguese also prudently followed the shoreline and kept a sharp eye for home-bound winds. The Chinese, despite the multiculturalist wish to accord Admiral Zheng-he and a non-Western country a place in the age of exploration, visited only previously known ports.[28]

Several other daring expeditions were attempted earlier, notably by two Portuguese sailors, Fernão Dulmo and João Estreito, who in 1487 sailed west never to be heard from again.[29] Reports of others sailing out of England and elsewhere were common in the late fifteenth century, but no one left a definite record of discovery and return. Most disappeared without even leaving their names to history. Clearly, such efforts show that an exploratory mood was growing in the European Atlantic, but they should not be read through the distorting lens of hindsight. The disappearances cannot help but have introduced further doubts and fears among those considering similar undertakings.

Columbus's marked and persistent certainty that he could reach the Indies has led to some speculation, based on rumors dating back to his own lifetime, that Columbus had rescued a ship-wrecked Portuguese sailor who told him about land in the west. The story appears to be false, and both his son and other sympathetic early commentators attribute it to the ill will of detractors. But even if it were true, the fact that no ship, so far as the principal countries of Europe knew, had ever returned from across the Atlantic would hardly have increased anyone's confidence to make the attempt.

God's Messenger

In the preface to the *Libro de las profecías* (Book of prophecies) he compiled near the end of his life, Columbus relates and perhaps exaggerates to Ferdinand and Isabella how he became convinced that the voyage was not merely possible but his own special vocation:

45

During this time, I have searched out and studied all kinds of texts: geographies, histories, chronologies, philosophies, and other subjects. With a hand that could be felt, the Lord opened my mind to the fact that it would be possible to sail from here to the Indies, and he opened my will to desire to accomplish this project. This was the fire that burned within me when I came to visit Your Highnesses.[30]

Adding that God wished there to be a *milagro ebidentísimo* (very conspicuous miracle) in this enterprise, Columbus repeats that he is an uneducated man; "for the execution of the journey to the Indies, I was not aided by intelligence, by mathematics, or by maps. It was simply the fulfillment of what Isaiah had prophesied."[31]

When Columbus mentions "a hand that could be felt," he is not speaking strictly metaphorically. At several critical points in his life, he seems to have even heard a "voice" speaking prophetically to him.[32] Early and late in life Columbus appears to have believed he had a calling from God to make his trip. It was not the first time in Western history that a man felt inspired by God to do one thing but, in the event, achieved another. Though commentators have long noticed Columbus's religiousness, it has not received proper treatment, and certainly has been misunderstood, until very recently. Most historians have accepted the religion as sincere, particularly when it manifests itself in the face of danger from storms. But Columbus's extensive writing on the subject is widely regarded as misguided and therefore unimportant. Yet it is an absolutely crucial element in understanding everything for which he is remembered.

His *Libro de las profecías*, which he assembled with the help of Gaspar de Gorricio, a monk from the Carthusian monastery at Las Cuevas, is a mass of scriptural and other texts that Columbus believed predicted his voyage to the New World. Akin to the mystical speculations of Pascal and the enormous commentary of Isaac Newton on Old Testament prophecies, this work is an embarrassment to Columbus's admirers[33] and a target for his detractors.[34] Practical men, men of a scientific bent, are not

46

supposed to indulge in these spiritual lucubrations. Along with late letters and other materials, the *Profecías* has usually been dismissed as evidence of a man whose mind has plunged back into mysticism in the worst sense of the word—understandable only as a reaction to the unpleasant realities of Columbus's closing years. The book was not even translated from the original Latin into a modern language until 1984.[35]

Though Washington Irving and many other major biographers knew of this text, it was long not accorded its proper value, perhaps owing to the myth of Columbus the progressive. In fact, the modern English translator and commentator on it, Delno C. West, found that the copy at Princeton's Firestone Library, which he first examined in the 1980s, still had the pages uncut.[36] West says of the importance of the text:

> The apparent inconsistencies in his story and action are not so much weaknesses and lapses as his own attempts at accommodation to political realities in a world in which his particular kind of motivation was rare and difficult to engage. He was a man of visions, dreams, hope. All of these goals were unintelligible to many of his contemporaries and to nearly all of his biographers and readers in the succeeding five hundred years. But the goals were perfectly clear in the light of his biblical sources and world events as seen through the eyes of prophecy.[37]

Though West's statement is a little too sweeping and perhaps sails a little too close to a conventional Columbus as Catholic saint, his work has uncovered essential and largely overlooked dimensions of the admiral and his relentless push toward the Indies.

Religious Enthusiasms

Columbus's growing obsession with religion shows unhealthy features. It has been suggested that physical or mental illness accounts for some of the more bizarre beliefs he came to hold. Modern pathologists have even diagnosed Columbus, probably correctly, as suffering from Reiter's syndrome, a severe rheumatoid arthritis.[38] But Reiter's syndrome, though it debilitates the sufferer periodically, does not produce mental instability. The fundamental question is: did Columbus's vision change late in his life? Or was he only emphasizing something in his thought and action that had always been present? West has discovered that among the notes in Columbus's handwriting at the back of the *Historia rerum ubique gestarum*, a popular medieval book about foreign lands by Aeneas Sylvius Piccolomini (later Pope Pius II), is "an earlier, smaller version of the *Libro de las profecías*."[39] The entries bear the date 1481, over ten years before the first voyage to the Americas. Columbus was only thirty at the time. Whatever developments his beliefs underwent, it seems indisputable that an apocalyptic vision guided Columbus from his early manhood on.

These early religious concerns show that his later professions were not merely a cover for Spanish imperialism and personal ambition, even though they were mixed up with both impulses. Scholarly opinion has come to recognize how deeply Columbus was influenced by medieval Franciscan traditions of the end times, particularly by those of the prophet Joachim of Fiore. Many New Testament texts predicted that the world would not end before the gospel had been preached to all nations. Columbus firmly believed that he was preparing the way for finally accomplishing this task. He knew from reading Marco Polo, for example, that out of curiosity about Christianity Kublai Khan had asked the pope to send missionaries to Cathay. Political and military turmoil had prevented the two priests assigned from completing their journey. Columbus's pressing forward and certainty about the nearness of Cathay resulted from his belief that he had been called on to finish that business.

Golden Means to Sacred Ends

These discoveries enrich our understanding of Columbus's relentless pursuit of gold. Like many of the Spanish who came to the New World, he sought profit, in the most tangible sense of the word, for himself and his descendants. Yet few accusations of raw personal greed surface in the many accounts we have of Columbus, some by his mortal enemies. Nor do his habits, despite the privileges he tried to secure, much reflect a man savoring the prospect of massive personal wealth. The Franciscans, the Catholic religious order most dedicated to the vow of poverty, were always hospitable and helpful to him in his petitions to important Spanish figures. Several recent students of Columbus's millennial vision have observed that when he traveled through Spain, he stopped at monasteries rather than the homes of caballeros or grandees.[40] During his later years Columbus's typical dress in Spain was indistinguishable from that of lay members of the Observantine Franciscans, an austere group within the Franciscans. No conclusive evidence exists that Columbus was a lay Franciscan, but these are just some of the indications that he was. The gold he sought, though partly intended for himself and his heirs, was mainly to be used for far different purposes and became bound up with what one historian has called a "spiritual quest."[41]

Though Columbus contrives to keep Ferdinand and Isabella interested in his "enterprise of the Indies" by emphasizing the beauty and wealth of the New World and the general friendliness of its inhabitants, he also frequently encourages them to use the wealth he has uncovered to mount a last crusade to retake the Holy Land. The long struggle to expel the Moors from Spain, which ended only in January 1492, kept the crusading spirit alive there longer than elsewhere in Europe. Furthermore, the Turkish conquest of Byzantium in 1453 had made all of Europe feel threatened. But Columbus had far greater aims in mind: that the Spanish king would complete the New Testament prophecies and usher in the end time.

Ferdinand himself seems not to have found the idea preposterous. In light of the Islamic threat, he took special pride in seeing himself as a crusading liberator and even coveted the title "King of Jerusalem." He submitted proposals for the conquest of Jerusalem to his Cortes. In this he may have been taking advantage of a mistaken belief, which Columbus accepted as true, that Joachim of Fiore had predicted the retaking of the Holy Land by a king of Spain. None of Joachim's writings, however, suggest Spain as the instrument of the final struggle. Various skeptical parties, including Machiavelli (who in *The Prince* regards Ferdinand as an exemplary and effective two-faced ruler), have argued that Ferdinand was not serious about these proposals.[42] According to this view, Ferdinand, confident that the Cortes would reject the idea, proposed the crusade to win credit for his good intentions.

The medieval preoccupation with crusades to retake the Holy Land may not be very intelligible to most modern readers. But this shows a blind spot in our intellectual vision. We find it hard to believe that religious motives in themselves can move people when they conflict with desire for power or wealth. Yet Iran in the 1970s and 1980s has acted against its own worldly interests in what it sees as adherence to religious principle. In 1494, just two years after Columbus's New World landfall, the Dominican monk Girolamo Savonarola came to power in Florence—then in the full flower of the Renaissance. Religious zeal led to bonfires of the beautiful vanities that we associate today with the very name of Florence.

Religious impulses have strong worldly consequences. Few people have any difficulty understanding, for example, why modern Jews desired and vigorously defend the state of Israel. Jews, like Christians, believe in a God who is simultaneously transcendent and the Lord of history. The special places where, and persons to whom, He has shown himself are not merely negligible vehicles but part and parcel of a Creator God. In fact, all the religions of the Book, including Islam, share the perception (which exists in different form among some non-biblical peoples as well) of sacred sites. The desire to possess, and to worship at, these sites is as natural as the Jewish desire for the biblically promised homeland.

Holy wars to capture such sites may seem improper to persons who believe religion should lead to pacifism or at least promote peace, but most of us can understand why peoples from various cultures show a special attachment and willingness to go to war to gain ancestral and sacred lands. The Old Testament certainly seems to support that kind of war under certain conditions; the ancient Hebrews had to defeat the Canaanites. Similarly, the founders of the modern Jewish state had to take Palestine by force. This enterprise, however, should be distinguished from the use of force in proselytizing, a practice that seems to have been countenanced without qualms only by Islam among the three faiths of the Book and even among Muslims only intermittently.

The crusades have gotten a bad reputation because of the human corruption that accompanied such an allegedly holy cause. As T. S. Eliot has portrayed the situation in his "Choruses from 'The Rock' ":

> Some went from love of glory,
> Some went who were restless and curious,
> Some were rapacious and lustful.
> Many left their bodies to the kites of Syria
> Or sea-strewn along the routes;
> Many left their souls in Syria,
> Living on, sunken in moral corruption;
> Many came back well broken,
> Diseased and beggared, finding
> A stranger at the door in possession:
> Came home cracked by the sun of the East
> And the seven deadly sins of Syria.

But Eliot concludes:

> Not avarice, lechery, treachery,
> Envy, sloth, gluttony, jealousy, pride:
> It was not these that made the Crusades,
> But these that unmade them.[43]

We are unused to this idea, but the medieval view is not simply irrational or corrupt.

At any rate, Columbus was willing to put his treasure where his heart lay. He made a will in 1498 before his third voyage that was later altered in various ways. But one point remained firm until his death: he directed the executors of his estate to set up a fund in Genoa's Bank of Saint George to help pay for the liberation of Jerusalem.[44]

Medieval and Not

While these religious passions clearly link him to medieval categories of thought, Columbus was willing to risk his life to show that some medieval lore was incomplete, false, or misconstrued. Columbus may have been medieval in a variety of ways, but there were some important ways in which he was not. Though he is committed to converting the world, for example, he is not rigidly intolerant. Even late in life he writes, "I believe that the Holy Spirit works among Christians, Jews, and Moslems, and among all men of every faith, not merely among the learned, but also among the uneducated."[45] Some of the "sweetness and benignity" of character mentioned by Las Casas shows itself here.

Nor does he greatly manifest the characteristic medieval superstition about imaginary terrors or boundaries beyond the known world. The experiences of a sailor, and also a certain type of religious mind, prevent him from accepting tall stories without corroboration. Some parties have accused him of credulity, or at least fanciful misunderstanding, in accepting the Taínos' stories that the Caribs were cannibals.[46] Though he is eventually convinced of their view, he resists that interpretation for quite a while. In several places in his *Log*, he says things such as this:

> The Indians with me continued to show great fear because of the course I was taking and kept insisting that the people of Bohío had only one eye and the face of a dog, and they fear being eaten. I do not believe any of this. I feel that the Indians they fear belong to the domain of the Great Khan.[47]

Whatever misunderstandings may be occurring in such early exchanges because of the language barrier (Columbus notes this difficulty as well), it is clear that Columbus does not arrive at his belief that the fierce Caribs were cannibals merely because he had read of *anthropophagoi* in ancient and medieval texts. And it appears his belief was correct. A modern biography adds: "To deny that cannibalism existed, one needs to assume that a wide range of European commentators simply made up the stories, an interpretation that defies reason, logic, and the available evidence."[48] Only in the log entry of January 13, 1493, after more than three months in the Caribbean listening to the fears of natives, does Columbus report Indian tales of cannibalism without some skepticism.[49]

Columbus's willingness to disregard certain medieval notions has led many people to see him as poised between the Middle Ages and the Renaissance. To them his search for wealth, station, and knowledge manifest the very characteristics that define the Renaissance shift to emphasizing the life of man in this world. Lending weight to this end of the scale is the fact that Columbus also had an artistic side. Las Casas says, "So fine was his hand that he might have earned his living by that skill alone."[50] His ultimate goal in compiling the book of prophecies was eventually to present the monarchs with an apocalyptic poem, of which we have some preliminary portions. Though by no means proof of a poetic talent of the first rank, the verses of this sailor-turned-explorer-turned-millenarian thinker add another dimension to an already complex man.[51]

Misrepresentations and Misunderstandings

Many historians and ideologues, however, overplay Columbus's Renaissance side for various reasons, usually having to do with modern agendas. His medievalism notwithstanding, he is made to stand as a symbol of the incipient European capitalist and even imperialist, with all the ignoble characteristics often associated with those figures.[52] This charge reflects a misrepresentation of and condescension toward both the Middle Ages and the Renaissance not easily compatible with the facts. The Middle Ages were not sedentary or self-satisfied or uninterested in profitable commerce by any means, merely limited by the knowledge and technology available until the fifteenth century. Medieval Venice and Genoa were the twin centers of Mediterranean naval commerce that paved the way for later commercial activities around the world. In *The Medieval Expansion of Europe*, J. R. S. Phillips shows that the push into the New World was a growth in the scale

53

of exploration but is better understood as a continuation of, rather than a new departure from, impulses already present in Europe for centuries.[53] Columbus personally, moreover, exhibits a Franciscan delight in nature and the goodness of creation very much at odds with the facile contemporary picture of him as the precursor of rapacious, environmentally damaging capitalism. For Columbus the New World was a kind of medieval *locus amoenus* in which human, animal, vegetable, and inanimate nature show a primitive harmony. That he did not anticipate the harmful effects of human use on the environment—effects that have become clear only in the last century or so—merely reflects the relatively small scale of enterprise in his time.

Even some of the best recent writers on Columbus cannot quite give up certain mental habits and prejudices in their views of history—an incapacity that, paradoxically, mirrors the limitations they attribute to Columbus. John Noble Wilford, in his generally lucid but badly titled *The Mysterious History of Columbus*, often succumbs to the clichéd opposition between medieval and Renaissance. Wilford's training as a science writer perhaps betrays him here. He contrasts the allegedly dogmatic Columbus who never relented in his belief that he was in the Indies, for example, with the Florentine humanist Amerigo Vespucci after whom America is named. Vespucci was from a noble family, and his vivid accounts of exploration were the primary vehicles through which the term New World came to be applied to the newly discovered lands. Wilford sees Vespucci as more of a Renaissance humanist than the Genoese admiral, as an "open-minded observer" who helps conceptualize the new situation.

This opposition of two contemporaneous figures reflects one of the subtler forms of bias that continues in Columbus studies. Tzvetan Todorov, a literary theorist who has concocted an elaborate and dubious history of European intellectual imperialism in the New World, has asserted that Columbus was medieval in everything not touching navigation.[54] In other matters he submitted to and argued from authority. Vespucci, in the spirit of the Renaissance, was an empiricist. But, contrary to what Todorov may think, the Renaissance itself was not primarily empirical. The rediscovery of antiquity shifted the appeals to authority to other texts in addition to Scripture (and the few Greek and Roman writers known to the Middle Ages). Such empiricism as began to develop was guided by ancient authors. Vespucci's empiricism is comparable to Machiavelli's, which is to say that both retreated from Scriptural categories to classical ones. Columbus and Vespucci both use the word continent for what is now South America. Columbus probably continued to believe that it was part of Asia; Vespucci's beliefs are also uncertain, though at times he seems to have made the breakthrough to the new conceptualization. The Mexican historian Edmundo O'Gorman has carefully traced the growing mental change caused by the new lands in his ingenious *The Invention of America.* He shows with clarity that neither figure unequivocally understood that they were exploring "America." That realization—and the host of implications it brought in its wake—came, perhaps, with Martin Waldseemueller's 1507 *Cosmographiae Introductio,* in which Vespucci's name is first applied to the New World.

What is at work here is a search for the roots of modern empiricism in the earliest European experience of the Americas, empiricism being one of the strongest currents in modern philosophy. But it is not very plausible that either Columbus or Vespucci fits the need. Vespucci is primarily a *litterateur* who writes well of the new sights; as such he has no grand theory of geography. His accounts are marked by a closed-mindedness of their own, for example, in his belief that the nakedness, promiscuity, and lack of political organization among native groups were evidence that they "live according to nature." This is as false—and European—a dogma as Columbus's medieval belief that all the continents are one divided landmass. The realization of the type of newness the Americas represented appears to have been the work of several minds rather than any one.

One of the oddest new approaches to Columbus makes use of esoteric postmodern literary theory to show how European language itself became a tool of conquest in the New World. In his critically acclaimed study *Marvelous Possessions*, Stephen Greenblatt argues that medieval astonishment at strange peoples and sights, which evoked puzzled respect for "the other," was transformed in the late fifteenth century into something wholly different. "Renaissance wonder" became "an agent of appropriation," reflecting a new desire for ownership and colonialism.[55] Greenblatt admits that what he calls "the language of Christian imperialism" did not *necessarily* promote appropriation, since religious figures like Las Casas and Francisco de Vitoria made anti-imperial religious arguments (see chapter three). But, he contends, in the European Christianity of the time, religious and worldly desires were readily "convertible."[56] For Greenblatt, Columbus was rarely a cynic, skeptic, or hypocrite. Rather, the admiral was a product of an increasingly pathological European culture that united religious aims and greed.[57]

Greenblatt's book is ingenious and careful in its reading of early-contact history. But for all its innovations and discoveries, *Marvelous Possessions* basically reproduces the old view that the Renaissance brought a rapacious spirit to bear on the physical world. It chides Europeans, moreover, for first reacting to different cultures the way people everywhere do — with misunderstanding and the use of familiar concepts to categorize the other. Except for its fine literary examination of a wealth of cultural and historical material, this analysis offers little that is new.

Bad in Any Case

Perhaps the traditional opposition between the medieval and Renaissance Columbuses is fading in the postcolonial and postmodernist world. In Kirkpatrick Sale, Columbus is uniquely and doubly condemned for being medieval *and* for being of the Renaissance. His medieval side reflects superstitions, and his Renaissance side shows the destructive force of naked instrumental and mathematical reason, which Sale largely identifies with Renaissance Europe. Nevertheless, Sale also feels free to castigate Columbus for his lack of interest in numbers, that is, for not giving us the exact mathematical coordinates of the island where he made first landfall. Poor Columbus is merely the product of various opposing evil traditions that define Europe and Europeans—of which we are all the heirs, save, of course, the Kirkpatrick Sales who transcend cultural determinism.

All these attempts at neat categorizations assume that we can define a man, as well as a historical period, with far sharper boundaries than is ever the case. The mixture of human weakness and human greatness in even a key figure is never easy to calculate. The novelist Anthony Burgess has recently created a Mozart who says, "My desire and my hope is to gain honor, fame, and money."[58] That sentence plausibly formulates a great deal of truth about Mozart's life. Yet few music lovers would deduce from this that Mozart's work is, therefore, solely the product of ambition and cupidity, or try to explain the man and his music by sociological analysis of the late eighteenth century. Columbus similarly spoke of "God, gold, and glory," and many of the Europeans who followed him were driven by multiple motives, not all of which were, by any means, merely self-serving.

Kirkpatrick Sale, as usual, well formulates the ultimate issue behind much of the public controversy over 1992:

> In the final analysis, it is not so important whether Columbus was a good man. What matters is that he brought over a culture centered on its own superiority. The failings of the man were and remain the failures of the culture.[59]

This is a strained argument. It certainly does matter, if only for the sake of historical justice, that we try to discern the mix of good and evil in Columbus *per se*. Furthermore, no one can simply be identified with a whole culture. Every individual both draws on and opposes elements in his surroundings. If the preceding pages show anything, they show that Columbus, like the rest of us, was not simply good or bad. As a great human spirit, both his virtues and faults appear larger and more vivid than they do in most people. And his historical influence reflects the dimensions of what he was. The argument about the European sense of superiority, however, can be engaged quite well without dragging in Columbus, as if he were a mere conduit for European culture.

One reason that freedom arose in the West is the traditional Western separation of the City of Man from the City of God. As we shall see in the next chapter, many of the early missionaries and theologians showed, in the very face of state power and financial interests, that Christian principles pointed toward other paths than those most often taken by settlers in the New World. Columbus and Las Casas were sometimes at odds over specifics, but were not fundamentally opposed on these matters. Las Casas is the greater figure for his moral passion and courage, but Columbus, in spite of his faults, deserves no little admiration. Emblematic, perhaps, of their relationship is the suggestion of Simón Bolívar in 1819 that a newly liberated area of South America be named Colombia and its capital Las Casas: "Thus will we prove to the world that we not only have the right to be free, but we will demonstrate that we know how to honor the friends and benefactors of mankind."[60]

3

Vox Clamantis in Deserto?

Spanish civilization crushed the Indian; English civilization
scorned and neglected him; French civilization embraced
and cherished him.

—Francis Parkman
The Jesuits in North America[1]

One of the most persistent and least examined strands in the
anti-Columbus myth is the charge that, in the decades
following 1492, missionaries and other religious groups did little
but sprinkle holy water on a brutally destructive imperialistic
conquest of native cultures. For the most part this mistaken
impression stems from simple, long-standing ignorance. Religious figures as diverse as Friar Bernardino de Sahagún in Mexico,
Roger Williams in Rhode Island, and the Jesuit Jean de Brébeuf in
New France were among the very first Europeans to learn native
languages and, in the process, to begin inventing the modern
disciplines of anthropology and ethnology. They also preserved a
good deal of what we know about several pre-contact native
cultures. Naturally, Christian evangelization of Indians raises
many large ethical questions, and not only on the European side.
While Christians had obligations to respect native cultural and
individual rights, most of us would agree that human sacrifice,
ritual cannibalism, slavery, and torture were native practices that
cried to heaven for change. On balance European religious institutions, far from being mere tools of colonialism, were often

59

among the strongest defenders of native life and culture in the New World.

To say this, however, we must remind ourselves of both the tragic and epic dimensions in this story. Once contact was established, native cultures would be changed forever. Just as the isolation of the Americas from the rest of the world made millions of deaths from disease inevitable—whether the first non–Native American arrived from Asia, Africa or Europe—so native religion and culture would have changed whether they first confronted Buddhism, Islam, Judaism, or Christianity. Though some revisionists have tried to equate Western religion itself with epidemic disease, the parallel is far from exact. Despite the complicity of religious individuals in some atrocities, Christianity in general was not a moral or spiritual pathogen. The proof of this is that few Native American religious systems could be revived in their entirety today without generating great controversy, even among Native Americans themselves. The heroic attempts by missionaries to bring more humane practices to very different and hostile peoples can no longer be seen in the pious images of the past. Yet there was an element of epic grandeur, mixed with baser elements, in that story.

Contemporary critics frequently assume that a general religious imperialism occurred analogous to the military imperialism—an assumption that neither the historical record nor many morally relevant facts warrant. Francis Parkman's view, quoted above, oversimplifies and even misrepresents the early history to a great degree. But it does suggest the need to examine at least three very different large-scale approaches to Native Americans, as well as diverse currents within each of the three, to arrive at an accurate picture.

The Religious Black Legend

Anglo-Saxon and Protestant bias against Spanish and French Catholics long colored criticism of the earliest missionary activity in the New World. For centuries various Protestant enemies of

Spain used information about Spanish atrocities in the New World—much of it provided by the Dominican friar and defender of the Indians Bartolomé de Las Casas and debated in remarkably open fashion by Spanish secular and religious leaders—to create the "black legend," a kind of catch-all for anti-Spanish propaganda. Lurid illustrations by artists like Theodor DeBry mixed with anti-Catholic slurs to create an image that, to this day, inspires prejudices about Spanish America. (Pro-Spanish advocates created a corresponding "white legend," listing all the benefits European culture and Christianity brought to the New World and excusing errors and atrocities on that basis.[2]) New France received slightly better treatment, but grudgingly. Parkman, that energetic but decidedly New England historian, feels free to tell his readers in an otherwise straightforward and fair report on the Jesuit missions to the Huron and other northeastern woodland tribes, "As for the religion which the Jesuits taught them, however Protestants may carp at it, it was the only form of Christianity likely to take root in their crude and barbarous nature."[3]

A double bias—against both allegedly benighted Catholics and allegedly benighted natives—appears clearly here. G. K. Chesterton once observed that much English history of the first Spanish explorations in the New World reflects "the desire of the white man to despise the Red Indian and the flatly contradictory desire of the Englishman to despise the Spaniard for despising the Red Indian."[4] While French Jesuits might fare somewhat better than their Spanish Catholic counterparts in Anglo-American histories, both are found inferior by even the fairest writers. Despite such biases, however, this older criticism did at least pay attention to facts, to the actual deeds and misdeeds of the first Europeans in the Americas.

A new, contemporary form of the black legend manifests no such virtue. Its proponents know few facts and, though profoundly influenced by the earlier prejudices, now condemn all European religious figures in the New World, Catholic and Protestant, Spanish and not. Most prominent native spokesmen and their supporters give the impression that Christianity and genocide are indistinguishable from one another and that all true Native Americans reject both. Oddly, though hundreds of thousands of Native Americans in the United States and tens of millions in Latin America seem happy to be Christians and to support their churches, even prominent church leaders have accepted this view.[5] As mentioned in chapter one, probably the most violently moralistic comment on the early role that Christianity played in the New World has come from the U.S. National Council of Churches (NCC). After an introductory page studded with several charges of genocide, rape, and "ecocide," the NCC's official resolution— *A Faithful Response to the 500th Anniversary of the Arrival of Christopher Columbus*—called for repentance, not celebration, and described the role of religion in the New World as follows:

> The Church, with few exceptions, accompanied and legitimized this conquest and exploitation. Theological justifications for destroying native religious beliefs while forcing conversion to European forms of Christianity demanded a submission from the newly converted that facilitated their total conquest and exploitation.[6]

The almost ritualistic repetition of "conquest and exploitation" in this brief passage and the equivocation about European forms of Christianity (what other forms were there at the time?) are indicative of several problems with this argument and many similar critiques of the missionaries who came soon after Columbus.

Facile Condemnations

Vast overreaching and a predictability born of lack of any real knowledge mar all such accounts. Stafford Poole, a close student of the early European religious activities in Latin America, has questioned, for example, whether genocide actually occurred:

> As elaborated in this century, the term applies to a calculated, deliberate extermination of an entire identifiable people for racial or other reasons. Despite the dreadful consequences of the European invasion of Latin America, there never was any

planned or calculated desire to destroy the people as such. . . . There are other terms to describe what happened in the Western Hemisphere, but genocide is not one of them. It is a good propaganda term in an age where slogans and shouting have replaced reflection and learning, but to use it in this context is to cheapen both the word itself and the appalling experiences of Jews and Armenians, to mention but two of the major victims of this century.[7]

Among the various early European settlements, only the English at Jamestown—and only some of them—ever seem to have contemplated extermination of Indians.[8] Certainly, no church group is recorded to have accepted such a course.

Furthermore, while missionaries may have accompanied conquerors, very few simply legitimized their actions. Unscrupulous and greedy churchmen may have sought their own advantage, but the nature of the religious vocation is such that those kinds of Christians are a small minority at any time. Quite a few religious leaders, especially in Spanish territories, clearly thought political dominance was a prerequisite to efficient evangelization, but that position did not entail blanket acceptance of everything Spaniards wanted to do. From the very beginning, religious scruple vied with worldly interests. The instances of *religious* imperialism in the most serious sense of forced conversion and gross mistreatment for heresy are not nearly as common—or unopposed—as is usually assumed.

Sailing on Columbus's second voyage, the first official representative of Christianity arrived in the New World in 1493. The priest Bernal Buyl was both apostolic vicar and a personal representative of Ferdinand and Isabella, who liked to style themselves *los reyes católicos* (the Catholic monarchs). When Columbus discovered that all the men he had left at La Navidad had been killed in his absence, Buyl advocated a hard line against the Indians. But Columbus chose, despite some troubling evidence, to believe the explanations of his old friend Guacanagarí that other tribes were responsible and to ignore Buyl. After a year of various conflicts with Columbus and other Spaniards in the New World, Buyl resigned and returned to Spain. His story, however, shows one pattern: religious rigor (Buyl) opposed to a mixed secular and religious leniency (Columbus). But other patterns—by no means exceptions to some harsh rule—also developed.

Serious religious debates began immediately over ethical conduct in the New World. Slavery, for example, was early opposed. J. H. Elliott, one of the premier historians of imperial Spain, points out that as early as 1500, theologians and others protested when Native Americans arrived on Spanish docks to be sold as slaves. This led Queen Isabella, who had already freed several Indians Columbus had sent back, formally to outlaw the practice. Not even a decade had elapsed since first contact with the New World.[9] Unfortunately, the legislation permitted exceptions— when Spaniards were attacked or when tribes practiced cannibalism, human sacrifice, or other crimes against natural law—that provided crude and unscrupulous people with numerous loopholes to do whatever they wished.

Anti-Spanish Bias

The NCC document, however, makes no mention of these reactions nor of the passionate and sophisticated defense of the natives and of native culture developed very early on by Spaniards, particularly in the Church—an omission that has not gone unnoticed by Hispanics.[10] As the American historian James Muldoon has commented:

> Hispanic critics of the NCC resolution have a point. The resolution was directed only at Columbus's voyages and, by implication, at the establishment of Spanish domination over much of the Americas. The English, French, Dutch, and even the Portuguese seem to have escaped this sweeping condemnation.[11]

In fact, the NCC seems blissfully unaware of the interesting and sometimes inspiring history of early Spanish activity in the New World, and the document—reflecting the organization's basic ideological thrust—does little more than repeat fashionable clichés about the "complicity" of missionaries in the oppression of native peoples then and now. It cites, vaguely, only two sources for these assertions, both clearly biased—*Black Elk Speaks* and Howard Zinn's *A People's History of the United States*.

This lack of curiosity about Christian history by a professedly Christian organization is telling and a grave moral failing. Had the authors of the statement gone outside their two meager counter-cultural sources, they might have discovered unfamiliar cultural and religious riches. They would have found a wealth of reflection on the nature of the native peoples and their cultures that would have helped them understand how Western cultures, precisely because of their encounters with Native Americans, gradually came to a more inclusive recognition of universal humanity. But the NCC appears to have been more interested in issuing a universal indictment of the West on the basis of prejudice against Hispanic culture.

Myopic Progressives

Defenders of the NCC statement and critiques like it contend that they are opening up Eurocentric history to alternative views. In fact, they present the most historically myopic visions imaginable. Not only are they ignorant of Native American cultures, their ignorance of Europe makes it impossible for them even to know what would, or would not, constitute a sinister Eurocentric view. A crucial issue in any history of the Americas is the origin of the concepts of universal human rights and respect for alien cultures that underlie contemporary critiques. We now take these principles for granted. But such concepts existed nowhere in the world prior to certain developments in Europe, least of all among non-Western cultures and New World tribes, who had their own versions of cultural superiority. Only because of some serious thinking in Western nations were the seemingly odd new peoples held to be rational—and therefore fully human—and international law developed to reflect that humanity. These were two new achievements even if practice followed theory very imperfectly.

65

To its credit Spain began grappling with these moral and philosophical questions almost immediately, though some confusion and disorder naturally attended the initial Spanish contact with the New World. The brutality and greed that arrived with the less-savory characters brought by later voyages compounded an already-difficult cultural problem. Columbus himself, as we saw in the previous chapter, did not know what to do about these developments other than to try to restrain the worst excesses and to beg the monarchs to consider carefully whom they were sending to the Americas.

Many of the missionaries also did not know at first what to make of this unprecedented situation. But in 1511, less than two decades after Columbus's first voyage, Antonio de Montesinos, a Dominican priest speaking on behalf of himself and two colleagues, denounced mistreatment of Indians in a homily given to outraged settlers on the island of Hispaniola. Montesinos pulled no punches. Invoking the biblical verse "I am the voice of one crying in the wilderness," he continued:

> This voice says that you are in mortal sin and live and die in it because of the cruelty and tyranny that you use against these innocent peoples. Tell me, by what right or justice do you hold these Indians in such cruel and horrible slavery? By what authority do you wage such detestable wars on these peoples, who lived mildly and peacefully in their own lands, in which you have destroyed countless numbers of them with unheard of murder and ruin. . . . Are these Indians not men? Do they not have rational souls? Are you not obliged to love them as you love yourselves? . . . In your present state you can no more be saved than the Moors or Turks, who do not have and do not want the faith of Christ.[12]

Montesinos's listeners in the pews, like many other settlers who would be chastised in the future by church and civil authorities, were predictably furious. He needed a protective escort to leave the church.

But in his fiery denunciation the priest was following and proclaiming the decree issued years earlier in 1503 by Ferdinand

and Isabella granting liberty to the Indians. The Mexican historian Rafael Altamira has said of that decree:

> What a memorable day for the entire world, because it signals the first recognition of the respect due to the dignity and liberty of all men no matter how primitive and uncivilized they may be—a principle that had never been proclaimed before in any legislation, let alone practiced in any country.[13]

The proclamation was mostly disregarded, but Altamira rightly pointed out that the appropriate response to such an early expression of good principles should be gratitude and surprise rather than condemnation for the limited effect those principles had in practice. Because we now assume that human rights are obvious and universal, we easily forget how much current standards owe to these first Spanish impulses.

Not only did the king and queen approve of Indian liberty, but two years earlier in 1501 they had instructed Governor Nicolás de Ovando about the Indians' religious life as well:

> Because we desire that the Indians be converted to our holy Catholic faith and that their souls be saved, for this is the greatest good that we can wish for, and because for this they must be informed of the matters of our faith, you are to take great care in ensuring that the clergy so inform them and admonish them with much love, and without using force, so that they may be converted as rapidly as possible.[14]

Reading these statements now, we cannot help but recognize that, however admirable, they were not enough to stop some horrible atrocities. Some critics dismiss the religious aims as a mere rationalization justifying imperial interests. Yet the record is clear that Seville took what practical steps it could to enforce its views of proper treatment of natives. Most contemporary critics of Christian evangelization, however, are simply unaware that such sentiments existed at all.

In fact, a fair study of the first half of the sixteenth century reveals a steady and growing ethical concern among the Spanish about how to understand and deal with the peoples of the New

World, who were so different from the Jews, Moslems, and Asians with whom Europeans were already familiar. Surprisingly humane legislation was regularly passed, if just as regularly ignored. Debates arose over factual and moral questions. Some colonists believed that the Indians were only beasts, incapable of governing themselves; others thought them fully rational and capable of self-governance.

Naturally some self-interest and personal rivalry played a role in these disputes. The first viceroy of New Spain, the shrewd and competent Antonio de Mendoza (who ordered the compilation of native history and native ways now known as the *Codex Mendoza*), advised his successor to circumvent all special interests with a simple practical rule:

> Treat the Indians like any other people and do not make special rules and regulations for them. There are few persons in these parts who are not motivated in their opinions of the Indians, by some interest, whether temporal or spiritual, or by some passion or ambition, good or bad.[15]

That early wisdom bore the seeds of impartial treatment for all, regardless of origin—a uniquely American tenet necessitated by the rich mixture of various peoples on these shores.

The Sacred and the Profane

In the decades after Columbus, little by little, Spanish authorities did promote such principles, often at religious prodding and at great risk. The first viceroy of Peru, Blasco Nuñez Vela, was killed by his own people when he attempted to implement the New Laws of 1542, which mandated protections for the indigenous population. In the early decades of the sixteenth century, laws had been passed prohibiting the Spanish from even using abusive names for the natives. While all this legislation demonstrated a basic good will, resistance by colonists, the vast distances involved, and lags in communication lasting months made governing the New World a difficult task.

But the laws and those charged with enforcing them were not always ineffective. When word of abuses reached the Spanish court, both secular and religious leaders were sometimes punished or recalled. The Emperor Charles V himself ordered one Francisco de Chaves to pay for the construction of an Indian school in recompense for mistreating Indians. And a far more notorious case involved the bishop of Yucatán, the Franciscan friar Diego de Landa. Landa was perhaps the most gifted linguist to study the Mayas in the early decades of European rule. Not only did he master the language, he recorded Mayan customs and history, becoming one of the most important anthropological sources for native culture at the time of first contact. Furthermore, his phonetic transcriptions of the words represented by Mayan glyphs— the only true writing in the New World—have been crucial to the recent successes in deciphering them. His missionary work, however, was overzealous. Landa tortured Indians he suspected of heresy and burned hundreds of Mayan books, which were lost forever. In 1564, following the outcry his actions evoked, he was recalled to Spain to stand trial.

Sadly, Landa and other missionaries failed at times to heed their own church leaders. Decades earlier, in 1537, Pope Paul III had stated authoritatively in the encyclical *Sublimis Deus* what was to be argued again and again for the rest of the century:

> Indians and all other people who may later be discovered by the Christians are by no means to be deprived of their liberty or the possession of their property, even though they be outside the faith of Jesus Christ; and they may and should, freely and legitimately, enjoy their liberty and the possession of their property; nor should they be in any way enslaved; should the contrary happen it shall be null and of no effect. . . . By virtue of our apostolic authority we declare . . . that the said Indians and other peoples should be converted to the faith of Jesus Christ by preaching the word of God and by the example of good and holy living.[16]

Contrary to usual assumptions that the Church simply forced conversions, the words gentleness and affability were frequently

invoked in various parts of the New World to encourage missionaries to adopt the most effective and Christ-like approaches to the
natives.[17]

The Defender of the Indians

The most significant New World religious figure in the first
century after Columbus was the Dominican friar Bartolomé de
Las Casas. Las Casas was only nine years old in 1493 when he saw
Columbus make his triumphant return to Seville from his first
voyage to the New World. The noble bearing of the admiral
impressed him, and the memory of that event remained with him
for the rest of his life. That life was intimately bound up with the
history of the Americas, particularly with protecting indigenous
peoples, a labor that earned Las Casas the title *defensor de los índios*
(defender of the Indians).

Las Casas was slow to arrive at this vocation, but when it came
upon him, it came with a vengeance. No trace of moral uneasiness
about Indian welfare seems to have troubled his early years. His
father and several uncles made the second voyage with Columbus,
and in 1501 Bartolomé and his father accompanied the newly
appointed governor Nicolás de Ovando to Hispaniola. But having
already begun his studies for the priesthood before he left for the
New World, Las Casas made his way back to be ordained in Rome
sometime around 1507. The next year he received an *encomienda*
—a grant of land and Indians to work it—in Cuba, and returned
there to a prosperous life as a priest. Though in theory the
recipients of *encomiendas* were required to watch over the physical
and spiritual welfare of the Indians, in practice they often treated
them as little more than slaves.

It was only a few years later that Las Casas suddenly found
himself overwhelmed by a desire to defend the Indians. He had
been acquainted with indigenous peoples since his father brought
him home a slave (freed by the decree of Isabella in 1500) and had
seen their mistreatment both on his early trips and in his capacity
as a chaplain in Cuba. But the first time he seems to have thought

seriously about the situation was after a Dominican priest refused him absolution during confession because he was holding Indians as an *encomendero*. In later years Las Casas would infuriate Spanish colonists with his *Confesionario*, a guide directing confessors to deny absolution to those who owned and abused native people.

The Dominican Order played a crucial role in the development of better relations with the Indians in the New World. Founded as a movement to teach and preach the truths of the Catholic faith, the Dominicans always recognized the need for "assiduous study." This requirement put them in the forefront of philosophical and theological thought. Two of the most prominent Dominicans, Albertus Magnus and Thomas Aquinas, made wide-ranging contributions to intellectual life in the High Middle Ages. And in the new era inaugurated by Columbus, the Dominicans continued to develop their particular fields of interest: they pondered deeply questions of justice, rights, and law in the new lands being conquered.

By contrast, most Franciscans and diocesan priests more readily accepted the necessity of Spanish military and political domination as a prerequisite to missionary activity. Generalizations about these issues, of course, leave out notable exceptions and nuances. Some Franciscans, too, thought and acted honorably in their own ways. And the Dominicans had serious differences of opinion. Las Casas himself became a Dominican in the 1520s, largely through the influence of Domingo de Betanzos. But he would later violently disagree with Betanzos, even questioning his motives, over whether Indians were sufficiently rational for self-government. Nevertheless, the most important *thinking* about right action in the New World and follow-up in political circles came almost entirely from Dominican figures. It is no accident that a Dominican brought the moral problems of the *encomienda* to Las Casas's attention in the confessional.

When first confronted, Las Casas meditated on his confessor's objections, but not until 1514, while he was preparing a sermon, did he come upon a text that brought him up short: "The sacrifice of an offering unjustly acquired is a mockery; the gifts of impious

71

men are unacceptable" (Ecclesiasticus 34:18). He announced from the pulpit the following Sunday that he was giving up his *encomienda*. From that moment on he became a tireless advocate of Indian rights.

Las Casas joined Montesinos in lobbying for Indians at the Spanish court. And their work met with some immediate success. Las Casas not only asked for and got some opportunities to try different approaches in the New World, he also influenced legal and theological debates in the Old. In 1530 he wrote a treatise, *De unico vocationis modo* (The only way of summoning), since lost, that argued persuasion was the only biblically correct method of preaching the gospel.[18] With Bishops Zumárraga and Julián Garcés he was able to send papers to Rome in 1536 that helped shape *Sublimis Deus*. His work was also instrumental, along with theological developments at the University of Salamanca, in framing the Spanish New Laws of 1542. But in 1550 he engaged in his most important battle: a theological dispute at the monastery of San Gregorio in the Spanish city of Valladolid.

The Importance of Valladolid

In that year the Spanish crown appointed a theological commission to come to some decision about the issues that had already long been debated about the natives in the New World. As Lewis Hanke, perhaps the most learned American analyst of the role religion played in the Spanish expansion, has pointed out, "For the first time, and probably for the last, a colonizing nation organized a formal inquiry into the justice of the methods used to extend its empire."[19]

Throughout the first half of the sixteenth century, religious figures had argued over the proper conduct of church and state in the New World. To us, human beings are human beings and have rights, and only wicked arrogance accounts for any questioning of their humanness. But until relatively recently no culture in the world—particularly none outside the European sphere of influence—widely accepted that understanding and put it into practice. Ironically, the much-maligned Spanish began the elaboration of these universal principles through theological reflection on indigenous peoples.

Charles V ordered the theological commission to hear the arguments at Valladolid and reach a conclusion. He also suspended any further military activity until the ethical questions were settled. During the previous decades some disputes had grown up within the religious orders themselves about whether natives were rational and could govern themselves. At Valladolid, Juan Ginés de Sepúlveda, a learned humanist and the most eminent living commentator on Aristotle's *Politics*, made the case that Indians were what Aristotle called "slaves by nature." They could be subjugated by Spaniards—but only for their own good and in the interest of rational government.

Our immediate reaction to this is—quite properly—revulsion. In the sixteenth century Sepúlveda did not find much intellectual assent either. His *The Second Democrates*, in which he first made these arguments, circulated in manuscript through the universities, where it was condemned almost universally.[20] Then as now, even among those who took Aristotle as a serious moral thinker, there was great uncertainty about what he meant by "slaves by nature"; who, if anybody, belonged in that category; and what were the grounds for deciding. Yet for all his intellectual arrogance and ignorance of the New World (Sepúlveda had never made the crossing), he had hold of a serious point that he argued crudely.

When we think of Indians today, we think of a weak, essentially benign group of peoples, badly treated for centuries, and this view colors our historical judgment. But the peoples and cultures of the New World before the spread of European influence differed widely from one another and did not always display characteristics that anyone would wish to defend today. Despite the special-pleading by defenders of Native Americans,[21] cannibalism existed without a doubt among the Aztecs, Guaraní, Iroquois, Caribs, and several other tribes. Pedro Fernandes Sardinha (Sardine), the unfortunately named first bishop of what is now Bahia, Brazil, for example, was eaten by the Caeté, a local tribe.[22] Human sacrifice was practiced by the high cultures and several groups not so developed. Slavery and torture were widespread from the Southern Cone to the Pacific Northwest. The cultural differences between Europe and the Americas were accented by the bloodshed and cruelty on both sides, and made mutual understanding difficult. If the Aztec Empire had been left alone and were still intact today, for example, most of us would argue that humanity and reason cried out for intervention in that culture. But the same was true of other indigenous groups, toward whom today almost everyone feels basic human sympathy.

Given circumstances like these, we should not be too quick to dismiss every argument in favor of Spaniards taking up the responsibility to govern natives as a sign of mere cynical opportunism. However wrong the anti-self-government position of Domingo de Betanzos, for example, he made a serious attempt to discern truth and responsibility.[23] Betanzos had not only led Las Casas into the Dominican Order, he had supported his early lobbying efforts on behalf of the Indians at the Spanish court. But with time and greater experience of the New World, Betanzos became less convinced of the wisdom of allowing Indians to govern themselves as they had before the Spaniards arrived.

Las Casas is the one figure whom even the most radical critics credit with a truly humane approach to indigenous peoples, but by no means did he stand alone. As has been discussed earlier, several religious and secular authorities also believed Indians warranted the same treatment as other men. But it was Las Casas who lobbied tirelessly for decades and made a massive theological defense of the Indians at Valladolid. Although the judges did not submit a final verdict on the Las Casas-Sepúlveda debate, the evidence of Indian rationality and the corresponding Spanish duties had been thoroughly and publicly presented for all fairminded people to examine. Las Casas cited examples of native government, art, architecture, sailing skill, and various other accomplishments, pointing out that these could not be regarded as the products of mere brutes.

In fact, it is a delicate ethical question whether in his zeal to

74

protect Native Americans Las Casas did not go too far. In 1963, around the four-hundredth anniversary of his death, at least one serious historian argued on the basis of modern psychological theory that Las Casas was a clinical paranoiac.[24] Certainly, there was no compromise in him; he decried his opponents as evil, never merely mistaken in their judgments. His passion was apparent in his obvious inflation of numbers and other exaggerations. While Sepúlveda briefly summarized his arguments for the theological experts at Valladolid, Las Casas went on obsessively—for days—with a torrent of testimony far beyond the capacity of his listeners to absorb. One of Las Casas's most extreme positions was that human sacrifice among certain native civilizations should not be taken as evidence of willful evil requiring harsh measures. For him this ritual practice reflected an ill-informed piety among natives who had no way of knowing better. Unlike Jews, Muslims, and Asians, he contended, natives in the Americas had been isolated from the rest of the world and had never had a chance to be guided by the revelation of the Old or New Testaments. Even Las Casas's ally, the theologian and legal theorist Francisco de Vitoria (another pivotal figure in the developing ethical reflections on issues raised by the Americas), disagreed with him on this point. Vitoria concluded that natural law demanded the protection of innocents.

Some critics have accused Las Casas of a certain coldness of feeling (*frialdad sensitiva*) in pursuing the defense of Native Americans so unswervingly. But others have seen in his approach a truly remarkable early attempt to understand native religion from the inside. The Mexican historian Teresa Silva Tena has suggested that Las Casas produced perhaps the most interesting sentence written by a Spaniard in the sixteenth century when he claimed that the human sacrifices, "even if cruel, were meticulous, delicate, and exquisite," and that they testified to fervent religious observances among the peoples who practiced them.[25]

The debate at Valladolid did not give the Spanish government the clear theological and moral conclusions it desired. In a sense, however, this did not really much matter. Las Casas's testimony

75

bore fruit. His central views, shared by many Dominicans in the New World and in Spain, slowly reshaped Spanish activity. The worst abuses of native peoples became less severe and more infrequent in the closing decades of the century.

New World Achievements

Meanwhile, in the Americas, the missionaries had not been either idle or simply legitimizing conquest. Quite often, in fact, they tried to set up Christian enclaves outside secular jurisdiction —a continuation of the old medieval rivalries between church and state. Schools existed where Indians learned Latin and writing, while Spaniards learned native languages and wrote down Indian history and cultural lore. Had the best missionary schools been allowed to go their own way, an even better cultural mix, benefiting both the Old World and the New, would have had a fair chance of emerging. Some early fruits of such integration were the Náhuatl-Latin herbal of Juan Badiano and Martín de la Cruz, and the Franciscan Bernardino de Sahagún's rich compilations of information about native culture. In fact, in later debates, native achievements in these schools and the accumulated cultural record were used as evidence of the Indians' rationality and, therefore, humanity. One product of missionary schooling, the learned native Antonio Valeriano, later became *gobernador* of Tenochtitlán (Mexico City).

In some complex ways a religious melding of cultures occurred also. The cult of the *Virgen de Guadalupe* spread quickly after 1531 when, according to tradition, the Blessed Virgin Mary appeared to an Indian named Juan Diego on Tepeyac, a hill north of the current Mexico City. That apparition became a religious and ethnic rallying point for the *mestizo* peoples of the New World that persists until today. For the Indians the Virgin came to replace one of their goddesses. Mary's image on Juan Diego's cloak shows a woman with delicate Indian features standing above symbols associated with the pagan past. In Mexico and much of the rest of Latin America, this appearance radically changed secular and religious history. Christianity was no longer simply arriving from without; it had become a creative energy arising from within native culture.

Unfortunately, the potential revolution in relations this religious development offered was partly lost because of the European monopoly on clerical leadership. The historian Robert Ricard has argued that "if the colegio at Tlatelolco [a seminary for native-born students in Mexico] had trained only one bishop for the country, the whole history of the Mexican church would have been far different."[26]

Vitoria and the Beginnings of Modern International Law

Defenders of the Indians had to achieve two objectives in the years leading up to Valladolid. First, they had to prove that the Indians were rational and deserving respect. Second, and no less important, they had to make sure that the law respected their dignity as rational beings. The Dominican friar and theologian Francisco de Vitoria performed the second task and is now generally recognized, along with Suarez and Grotius, as one of the founders of modern international law.

Revulsion at Pizarro's conduct in the conquest of Peru first stimulated Vitoria's thinking about Spanish conquests in the New World, but he was soon carried by the very force of his thought to examine a whole gamut of issues relating to the widely differing and previously unknown peoples. Though Vitoria's contributions in this field are enormous, few know the extent and nature of the principles he elaborated. In *The Conquest of Paradise*, for example, Kirkpatrick Sale quotes Vitoria only once: "the imperfect creature falls to the use of the perfect." Sale means to suggest, wrongly, that Vitoria—and a long European philosophical tradition—sanctioned imperialism and ecological exploitation.[27] Vitoria did write this sentence, but anyone familiar with scholastic philosophy will recognize immediately that this familiar formula from Aristotle is hardly a justification for brutal imperialist politics. In fact, Vitoria's work led in a far different direction.

77

Basing his arguments on the best legal and moral authorities in the scholastic tradition, particularly Aquinas, Vitoria proceeded to develop principles of international law that became crucial to the universal recognition of the rights of all human beings. In the very heat of conquest and colonization, Vitoria contended that the Europeans had no right at all to take land already under cultivation and inhabited by natives. Vitoria was a distinguished theologian and a Dominican priest, but even a man with his reputation could not have been entirely safe from potential reprisals. His stand took courage, and the Spanish crown, to its credit, often asked him to sit on deliberative councils about the Indies.

Vitoria's formulations in various writings give an idea of precisely how simplistic and ill-informed is the impression created by Sale's single quotation:

—Every Indian is a man and thus capable of attaining salvation or damnation.

—The Indians may not be deprived of their goods or power on account of their social backwardness, nor on account of their cultural inferiority or political disorganization.

—Every man has the right to truth, to education, and to all that forms part of his cultural and spiritual development and advancement.

—By natural law, every man has the right to his own life and to physical and mental integrity.

—The Indians have the right not to be baptized and not to be forced to convert to Christianity against their will.[28]

So much for the simple domination of perfect over imperfect beings.

Believing that native peoples had full human rights, Vitoria did allow, however, that Europeans could occupy land not already claimed by Indians, provided they did no harm to nearby natives. This restriction may seem of little significance in light of what happened to native territories, but it is worth keeping in mind that the Treaty of Tordesillas (1494), proclaimed by no lesser a figure than the pope, had crudely divided the new lands between the

Spanish and Portuguese without concern for who might already inhabit them. Vitoria sought not only to restrain the crown and the colonists, but to alter a decision by the highest religious authority in the Christian world on the basis of Christian principles. He went even further; Vitoria argued that the pope should never have made such a treaty because, just as the emperor had no absolute right to rule everywhere, the pope had no universal temporal jurisdiction.

Some further principles of Vitoria's are worth quoting:

—The Indian rulers, whether natural or elected, enjoy the same fundamental rights as a Christian or European prince.

—According to natural law, a non-Christian cacique or king does not lose his dominion or jurisdiction due to his infidelity or idolatrous practices, and even Christian subjects are obligated to obey him.

—The Indian peoples may defend themselves with arms and may rebel against foreigners who unjustly seize their territories or who govern the republic to their own advantage or to the advantage of their own people.

—The Spaniards may justly defend themselves against belligerent Indians so long as they stay within the limits of legitimate defense; but they may not use victory as an excuse for seizing the Indians' towns or for enslaving their inhabitants; a properly defensive war does not justify conquest when the Indians believe, on account of ignorance, that they are justly defending their property.

—However, recourse to war and to said security measures may never serve as a pretext for slaughtering, or sacking or occupying the towns of the Indians, who are by nature fearful and humble, and who have more than sufficient reason for distrusting the Spanish conquistadors, whose ways are strange to them and who are armed and more powerful than themselves.[29]

Anyone familiar with just-war theory will recognize that Vitoria is here applying its principles of self-defense, just cause, discrimination, proportionality, and last resort to Spaniards and Indians equally. His awareness of the many difficult and delicate questions that had to be faced—to say nothing of the self-serving interpretations of principles to which the Spaniards were prone—makes this strong attempt at equality all the more striking. Writing in the 1530s with several decades of New World history available to him, Vitoria admitted few reasons, and those mostly in theory, for Spaniards taking over the governorship of natives. Prominent among those reasons were the protection of innocents from human sacrifice and cannibalism, and native blocking of peaceful evangelization.

Alarm bells go off for many modern scholars who read such exceptions, but they went off for Vitoria too. He argues in many passages that these exceptions are probably only theoretically possible, not likely in actual fact. Furthermore, he warns that unscrupulous men are apt to use these good principles for evil ends, and that the monarch should therefore be very careful about authorizing any military action.

In applying universal human concerns to specific political situations, Vitoria recommends the classical virtue of prudence. He puts himself in a long line of distinguished scholastic thinkers when he writes, "For the common good and in order to achieve greater harmony and peace among people, the ruler may licitly tolerate laws and customs that go against natural law."[30] While Spain has an obligation to reform inhuman practices gradually, "Spain's right to remain in the Indies with the intention of overseeing and governing the natives is acceptable only because of the need for change there and only on the condition that their reform and protection be carried out to the benefit and development of indigenous peoples."[31]

Perhaps the most important strain in Vitoria's thinking was his insistence that difference of religion alone could not justify resort to war. (In rare cases, blocking peaceful evangelization might justify war, since it violated natural liberties.) Not only does Vitoria place the weight of his own reputation behind this principle, he cites Thomas Aquinas and other doctors of the Church, and adds, "I know of no one of the opposite way of thinking."[32]

Vitoria treated these subjects primarily in two small collections of lectures that have been published under the titles *De Indis* and *De Iure Belli*. James Brown Scott, the most distinguished English expositor of Vitoria, has said, "In the lecture of Vitoria on the Indians, and in his smaller tractate on War, we have before our very eyes, and at hand, a summary of the modern law of nations."[33] Vitoria himself said modestly but truly of the lectures, "The whole of this controversy and discussion was started on account of the aborigines of the New World, commonly called Indians, who came forty years ago into the power of the Spaniards, not having been previously known to our world."[34]

Vitoria's positions develop the best of the prior Western international-law tradition in the face of a new challenge. Many of the passages above show the beginnings of principles we take for granted in international forums today. Vitoria is far closer to being an advocate of what is good in the Universal Declaration on Human Rights than he is to being Kirkpatrick Sale's fictitious theorist of cultural and environmental domination. Even more important for the history of the Americas is that Vitoria and his school at the ancient and prestigious University of Salamanca sent disciples throughout the New World.[35] As Doctor Samuel Johnson, a Tory critic of European arrogance and imperialism, was to say centuries later, "I love the University of Salamanca; for when the Spaniards were in doubt as to the lawfulness of their conquering America, the University of Salamanca gave it as their opinion that it was unlawful."[36]

Black Robes

Much further afield from the immediate impact of 1492 is the story of the Jesuit missions in New France during the seventeenth century. Several serious studies have adequately described the mixture of idealism and heroics, error and failure, that characterized the Jesuit missionaries.[37] They have had their rabid partisans and severe critics, no lesser a figure than Pascal joining the latter group in his *Pensées*. Yet the Jesuit record is essential to understanding both the diverse ways in which European Christianity inter-

acted with Native American culture and the later religious consequences of Columbus's voyage to the New World.

Early New France was not so much a colony as a trading post
for furs and other items valuable to Europeans and Indians alike.
As a result, conflicts over land claims and occupation did not play
as great a role there as they did in the early history of British and
Spanish America. Missionaries, too, were affected by this situation. Instead of being able to follow European settlements or
military exploits, the French Jesuits had to go out and live among
Indian tribes essentially unprotected. This took no little courage
because, as they doubtless knew, in Spanish America missionaries
unprotected by arms, no matter how peaceful in their approach to
Indians, had almost always been murdered.

Rather than forcing "European forms of Christianity" upon
native tribes, as some charge all missionaries did, the Jesuits in
New France, like their counterparts in China, sought to present
Christianity in native terms and forms. They found in the rituals
and beliefs of the main Eastern Woodland groups—Algonquian,
Huron, and Iroquois—parallels with Catholic sacraments and
dogmas amid other, less-congenial material. Unlike Protestants
who saw in nature only unredeemed and fallen humanity, the
Catholic system taught that grace builds on nature. The "black
robes," as the Indians called the Jesuits, tried to take advantage of
these natural affinities.

The Jesuit *Relations*, yearly reports back to the head of the
society in France, are a gold mine of early-contact material.[38] In
spite of the misunderstandings they contain and prejudices they
perpetuate (they were widely read in seventeenth-century France),
we have no more comprehensive source of information about
native culture and religion in the Northeast region. Though the
crudeness of some interpretations might make a modern anthropologist wince, a fair observer would have to say that the Jesuits
truly tried to understand, according to their lights, the peoples
they lived among.

Several of their discoveries remain of great interest. Some tribes
had legends resembling the story of the Fall, even including a

woman who tempted her husband with the fruit of a tree. Tales of a great flood and of a primeval man killing his brother also echoed the Bible. The Hurons and the Iroquois seemed to have had a more-developed concept of the afterlife than the Algonquins in the region. Whatever their scientific value, these detailed findings show what attention and care went into the first contacts.

And that sensitivity persisted and continues to have repercussions. As late as 1724, Joseph Lafitau, another Jesuit who lived among Indians for several years, was making careful studies of native culture and claiming that his discoveries had proved doubly enlightening. While his knowledge of the ancient Greek classics, particularly of the religious rites in Homer, had given him insights into Indian rituals, his familiarity with "the customs of the Savages afforded . . . illumination the more easily to understand and explain several matters to be found in ancient authors." Lafitau's observations are still of value today and have influenced the classical scholarship of the distinguished modern cultural historian Pierre Vidal-Nacquet.[39]

The Jesuits' work also required a great deal of bravery. Paul le Jeune, one of the earliest missionaries, remarked in 1632 on the "shocking cruelty to captives" among the warring tribes.[40] Seventeenth-century France, like the rest of Europe at the time, was not exactly unfamiliar with torture and executions, but the Frenchmen found native treatment of prisoners excessive even by those standards. Isaac Jogues, who himself was later tortured and killed, recorded one instance of what he thought was human sacrifice, a debatable but not wholly implausible construal of what went on at times among the Iroquois.

To get a concrete sense of the world in which the Jesuits operated and the practices they sought to change, it is instructive to recall what happened to Jean de Brébeuf. Brébeuf was a talented linguist who learned several Indian languages. Like many of the Jesuits, he was constantly having to defend himself from Indian charges of sorcery. (Even writing and reading were so alien to native ways of thought that they evoked fear.) Naturally, many Indians believed that sorcery was the cause of the epidemics brought by the French.

83

Brébeuf was working among the Hurons, tending the sick and trying to teach Christianity, when he was captured along with his colleague Gabriel Lalemant by the Iroquois. They tortured him to death, in steps: (1) Boiling water was poured over his head three times in imitation of baptism. (2) Hatchets were heated in a fire, strung together, and then placed around his neck. (3) A belt of resin and burning pitch was attached around his waist. (4) His lips and tongue were cut off. (5) Pieces of his own flesh were cut off, roasted, and eaten in front of him. (6) His heart was dug out and eaten. (7) His blood was drunk. Whatever shortcomings the Jesuits may have had, it is difficult not to admire, as the torturers themselves did, the courage they brought to a seemingly hopeless enterprise.

It is worth pausing a moment here on the question of cannibalism. A prominent scholar of Native American culture, Alvin M. Josephy, has argued in the introduction to a recent book he edited, *America in 1492: The World of the Indian Peoples Before the Arrival of Columbus*, that Columbus foolishly believed the Taíno tales of Carib cannibalism because of medieval superstition. But other contributors to the volume show that the practice was widespread even among the Caribs,[41] and Josephy himself admits as much by making the astonishing assertion that the Indian practice of eating the flesh of brave captives paralleled in religious meaning the Christian sacrament of the Eucharist. In this view the participants in both rituals desire to attain power and unite with a strong being. While such an aim may, in a general way, be common to both, the fundamental confusion about significant differences here is extremely misleading.

Christians never ate actual human flesh, nor does their sacrament involve the torture and death of another human being. They believe that God himself chose to suffer and submit to death. Although echoes of human sacrifice and cannibalism may still exist in Christian sacraments, it is a disservice to both real native beliefs and Christian teaching to conflate them. Brébeuf saying Mass and his Iroquois torturers do not have the same moral status. No one thinks that eating consecrated bread and drinking consecrated wine in church on a Sunday morning is a crime against universal human rights. Torture and cannibalism are such crimes. However much we may try to understand the meaning of these acts from the standpoint of someone within a native culture, we would not take a casual attitude toward them if they were still regularly occurring. In fact, we would agree on suppressing them, whatever the damage to native culture.

The Jesuit missions bore little fruit. The Hurons were converted and subsequently wiped out by a combination of disease and tribal warfare. Several Jesuits died horribly trying to present Christianity to native peoples in terms they could understand. Of course, other Christians were neither so delicate nor so heroic. But when we speak glibly of forced conversions and imposing European Christianity on native peoples, it is only fair to honor a group—one of several—that did neither and at least attempted a culturally sensitive approach, while showing an astonishing willingness to pay any price to make its efforts succeed.

Puritans and Nature

The ways in which the British brought Christianity to the New World are more complex. Unlike the Catholic Church, British Protestantism had no missionary orders and was riven by post-Reformation factions. The Puritans of Plymouth Colony looked upon themselves as a new saving remnant, reminiscent of the ancient Israelites who had gone out of Egypt into the wilderness. The colonists of Massachusetts Bay still felt themselves tied to the Church of England, a link that played no small role in Roger Williams's dissent and departure for Rhode Island. Quakers were burned as heretics in Massachusetts and eventually founded a colony of their own in Pennsylvania. Catholics led a precarious existence in Maryland. Virginia settlers wavered between Anglicanism and Puritanism. Under the circumstances it is not surprising that there was little organized effort to convert Indians.

Tricks and force may have later been used to make Indians Christians, but such practices did not characterize the earliest

English settlements. Puritan ideology made it difficult to arrive at a definite conception of who the Indians were. Were they a lost tribe of Israel, or were they merely unregenerate heathens like the Canaanites in the Old Testament? At least those few Puritans who occupied themselves with the Indians took the Indians as they found them. John Eliot, for example, showed true commitment to proper evangelization in learning indigenous languages (he translated the Bible into an Algonquian dialect) and in trying to convert natives through patient instruction. Understandably, Indians often fled Puritan religious talk, but that only shows they were free to do so.

The debate in English circles was not primarily, as among the early Spanish, about whether natives had rational souls. That issue, perhaps owing to the precedents set by the Spanish theologians, seems to have been settled in Puritan minds in the natives' favor. Daniel Gookin, an early Puritan missionary, probably expressed a typical sentiment, however, when he said that, except for their rational souls, Indians were "like unto the wild ass's colt, and not many degrees above beasts in matter of fact."[42] To Puritans the Indians seemed the very image of men without true religion and civilization.

Nevertheless, to their credit, at least some of the English sought to remedy this situation. Though John Eliot's labors were poorly supported by a community that had more pressing concerns, he did manage to arrange some instruction for promising young Indians, even university training at Harvard. Among the documents establishing that university, there is an allowance for "All other necessary provisions that may conduce to the education of the English and Indian youth of this country in knowledge: and holiness."[43] Though this inclusion of Native Americans was more a matter of theory than of practice, one Indian did take a B.A. at Harvard before 1700.

Other early British settlements adopted differing attitudes toward Indians. Roger Williams, like Eliot, learned native tongues and even wrote a guidebook, *A Key into the Language of America* (1643). Williams tried to keep on good terms with Indians, a desire largely upset by King Phillip's Rebellion in the 1670s. In general, however, Parkman is probably correct that the English mostly "scorned and neglected" Indians. If some of their basically respectful religious initiatives had generated more financial and social support, subsequent U.S. history might have been far different.

An Appraisal

When all is said and done, Vitoria, Las Casas, the Jesuits, the English missionaries, and other Christian groups did not have the full effect they might have had on behavior and evangelization in the New World. In part, this failure reflected the usual conundrum of human history—vices gaining the upper hand and ethical principles lagging far behind. In part, too, it reflected the sheer difficulty Spain, France, and England had in understanding and governing the New World over such vast and watery distances. Hasty and overzealous religious did not help the situation, more-over, with their superficial baptisms and insensitive impositions. And a moral lacuna remained for even the best representatives of Christianity: African blacks were sold into slavery without very much of the moral indignation raised by the mistreatment of Native Americans.

But the contact with native peoples planted a seed among religious thinkers, which was later to bear fruit in European culture as a whole. The Peruvian novelist Mario Vargas Llosa has argued:

> Father Las Casas was the most active, although not the only one, of those nonconformists who rebelled against the abuses inflicted upon the Indians. They fought against their fellow men and against the policies of their own country in the name of the moral principle that to them was higher than any principle of nation or state. This self-determination could not have been possible among the Incas or any of the other pre-Hispanic cultures. In these cultures, as in the other great civilizations of history foreign to the West, the individual could not morally

question the social organism of which he was a part, because he existed only as an integral atom of that organism and because for him the dictates of the state could not be separated from morality. The first culture to interrogate and question itself, the first to break up the masses into individual beings who with time gradually gained the right to think and act for themselves, was to become, thanks to that unknown exercise, freedom, the most powerful civilization in our world.[44]

That civilization owes no little debt of gratitude to the first Christian missionaries in the New World.

4

Multiculturalism, Europe, and 1492

> Whatever the particular crimes of Europe, that continent is
> also the source—the *unique* source—of those liberating
> ideas of individual liberty, political democracy, the rule of
> law, human rights, and cultural freedom that constitute our
> most precious legacy and to which most of the world today
> aspires.
>
> —Arthur M. Schlesinger, Jr.
> *The Disuniting of America*[1]

The nature of many elements involved in the study of 1492—
European colonialism, exploitation of natural resources, and
confrontation with pre-modern civilizations—made it perhaps
inevitable that Columbus would be drawn into the contemporary
debate over multiculturalism. Multiculturalism, as anyone familiar
with contemporary disputes about school and college curricula
knows, is the attempt to give equal place in education and therefore in society as a whole to allegedly marginalized groups.
African-American, Native American, feminist, homosexual, and
environmental perspectives should replace the dominant para-
digm, which is reviled as primarily white, Eurocentric, male,
heterosexual, and exploitative. The study of dead white European
males must give way to the study of other cultures and their
distinguished members. To the multiculturalist's eye Columbus
symbolizes everything that cries out for repudiation. In fact,
standing as he does at the very gateway to the Europeanization of

89

the Americas, Columbus has come to represent for some people the most wicked dead white European male of all.

Despite its widespread currency, multiculturalism remains a murky concept. In theory, the word suggests a substantive pluralism, a quintessentially American culture of cultures in which no voice predominates—save the voice that says no voice shall predominate. Absorbing and valuing contributions by various groups is a hallowed tradition in the United States, which has tried hard and been remarkably successful in holding together people from vastly different backgrounds. In practice, however, multiculturalism has often distorted the study of both the mainstream culture and peripheral groups by subordinating a complex social mosaic to a contemporary political agenda.

Indians as Environmentalists?

The usual form the multiculturalist argument takes is, first, to identify some obvious problem in contemporary American society and, then, to posit a non-European culture as possessing the solution to that problem. This method enables the multiculturalist to enlist support both from disgruntled members of mainstream society and from the generally small groups regarded as outside the European tradition. A staggering, industrialized United States is invited to look to Native Americans, for example, as models of good ecological behavior. But the evidence for this assertion is, at most, slender. The most often cited sign of Indians' environmentalism is their belief that it was necessary to ask a tree's pardon before cutting it and an animal's pardon before killing it. North American Indians did seek such permission but not for identifiably environmentalist reasons.

Though it is difficult and hazardous to generalize about such diverse peoples, Native American tribes probably did not even possess the idea of nature as a whole, a concept that appeared in the West only with the pre-Socratic philosopher Heraclitus. Native American religions did not present sharp distinctions between the spiritual and physical worlds. And it would be projecting Western categories upon their thinking to regard this undifferentiated, non-Western way of looking at reality as implying that all of nature was somehow sacred. Åke Hultkrantz, a student of Native American religion, has remarked that some contemporary Indian pronouncements make it

> sound as if the whole universe, particularly the natural environment, is sacred. This is not so; if it were, Indians would not point out certain stones, mountains, and lakes as sacred. Conservationists have mistakenly assumed that Indians are ecologists because they supposedly care for all of nature. In fact, there are many proofs of the devastation of nature by Indians.[2]

What Westerners regard as Indian respect for nature focused on some particular animal, plant, or place that might manifest the spirits of what was thought needful for human life. Making use of that thing might drive away or offend a spirit who had to be appeased, as the object was taken, in order to avoid wounded prerogatives and dire consequences. Indeed, fear of the spirits and of the physical world, which played a large role in native life, has very little, if anything, in common with our contemporary concern for the balance of nature.

Anyone who studies North American Indian cultures seriously will find interesting and complex peoples and, in many respects, an intriguing natural charm. But a thorough student will also come to realize that the Indians could not afford to indulge Romantic fantasies about what we call nature; they knew only too well that their environment could be as cruel as it was kind. They tried, as best as they were able, to bend nature to their use. Critics often denounce white culture as utilitarian, but Indian cultures were (and are) utilitarian as well. Among many Indians, Hultkrantz has found,

> we seek in vain for a pure aesthetic beholding of nature. An educated Senecan Indian well initiated into the traditions and values of his people once told me of the widely divergent reactions of Indians and whites when they move to new regions. The white man, he said, is impressed by the appearance of the

landscape and meditates over its beauty, whereas the Indian first of all asks, where are my medicines?[3]

Hultkrantz also observed that this same Indian, whom he met in Scandinavia, did not wax lyrical, as do Europeans, at the return of warm weather in spring. Western sentiment about nature over the last few centuries arose in large part from relative security and strength vis-à-vis natural powers. Confidence enables us to enjoy nature and appreciate its order because it is no longer such a harsh and, at times, overwhelming adversary.

At least some Indians take a much less Romantic view of nature than do modern environmentalists. Hultkrantz speculates that the contemplation of nature common among European peoples since the Romantics was a mode of thought unknown to the pre-contact Indian:

> Just as little as they performed art for art's sake—it was always a part of their technological, social, and symbolic activities— did they pursue a contemplation of nature to satisfy their aesthetic 'needs.' Their cultures simply did not provide for such needs.[4]

Paradoxically, the frightening success of Western technology has induced some Westerners and even some Indians to adopt extreme, near-quietistic stances toward nature. In a famous and often-quoted interview in the late 1890s, for example, a Shahaptin Indian of Washington State, reacted to the suggestion by whites that the tribe cultivate the land with this declamation:

> You ask me to plow the ground! Shall I take a knife and tear my mother's bosom? Then when I die she will not take me to her bosom to rest.
> You ask me to dig for stone! Shall I dig under her skin for her bones? Then when I die I cannot enter her body to be born again.
> You ask me to cut grass and make hay and sell it, and be rich like white men! But how dare I cut off my mother's hair?[5]

Extreme environmentalists take this statement as proof of a profound and universal Indian reluctance to disturb nature. But

92

anyone familiar with the various native tribes of North America knows that agriculture, mining, and harvesting went on for centuries among them. The Shahaptin's statement was a late reaction to white dominance more than an accurate representation of native belief. But this kind of distortion is quite common among those who wish to find their own modern beliefs reflected in native traditions. The utopian desire for undisturbed land tempts some whites to think that even using minerals somehow violates the sacred order of nature—which they assume does not admit of rational human needs.

Balances and Imbalances

In fact, even explicit Indian ideas of human harmony with nature do not necessarily offer comfort to a modern ecologist. When Indians wanted to cut trees, for example, they felt obligated to give the spirit to whom the trees belonged something in return, lest he grow angry and remove all trees. In many tribes the spirit was offered tobacco, and then the trees were cut. We usually conflate this religious practice with the modern wish to preserve, enjoy, and respect nature, but such an image may be very wide of the mark. In purely physical terms these religious practices could lead to great damage. "In theory the Iroquois were conservationists," William Fenton has said, but in practice they "often contributed to the decline of species." They broke off entire tops of trees to harvest cherries and, even before the white man's arrival, probably overhunted deer and beaver.[6] Significantly, because of the way they exhausted resources, small native bands like the Iroquois had to move their villages approximately twice per generation.[7]

While it might be edifying for our desacralized and industrialized culture if modern environmentalists followed Indian customs and prayed before acting, it would not disguise the evidence that, even in the thinly settled region of the North American Woodland cultures, Indians often exhausted the resources of a certain area and then moved on. The difference between them and, say, a

93

modern paper company was that they were few enough—and land plentiful enough—that their actions threatened few major or long-term consequences. Today, in fact, paper companies will take steps to replant a forest, if for no other reason than economic self-interest. But such conscious care could not exist without a certain understanding of the physical world that was only partly present to Native American peoples.

That understanding was not apparent among more developed native civilizations either. The shortcomings in their own relationship to nature had more far-reaching, visible consequences than did those of their woodland counterparts. For a long time archaeologists believed that the Mayas—a developed, urban people—were gentle, scholarly astronomers. It was only with the gradual success in deciphering Mayan glyphs, the one true writing system among Native Americans, that they learned otherwise. The great Mayan city-states in Mesoamerica abruptly collapsed about six hundred years before Columbus arrived in the Americas, their people returning to a much lower level of material culture. No one is sure exactly why this happened, but exploitation of and stresses on the environment seem to have been major factors. The evidence suggests that the Mayas regressed owing to their exhaustion of the tropical forests, as well as to endemic warfare among their city-states, epidemics, and political turmoil.[8] Whatever harmony with nature that may have existed among the Mayas appears to have been, as in other cultures with which we are familiar, hit and miss and profoundly subject to the human propensities toward evil and error.

Likewise, roughly about the time Columbus arrived in the Caribbean, the great Cahokian mound-builder culture of southern Illinois simply dispersed itself, probably *mutatis mutandis* for similar reasons. It is not unreasonable to speculate that weakness made the more primitive Native American tribes somewhat ecologically benign, and the more advanced Native American civilizations showed pathologies as bad as, or worse than, those in other developed civilizations. While the plagues, wars, and famines of

94

medieval Europe may show a civilization in turmoil, for instance, none of these natural and man-made disasters led to a decline in European society comparable to that of the Mayas or mound-builders.

Varieties of Harmony

The Native American pathologies could be very bad indeed, and not only for environmental reasons. Many modern Westerners who blithely invoke the image of indigenous peoples living in harmony with nature and with one another regard Christianity and Judaism as having inherited from the Bible a uniquely evil injunction to "subdue and dominate" the earth.[9] Other cultures, they believe, had religious principles that demonstrated reciprocal and harmonious relationships with the physical world.

But reciprocity and harmony are equivocal terms. In different cultures they may not necessarily result in what we would recognize as the good, the true, or the beautiful. For Algonquians, Iroquois, and other groups, kidnapping one another was part of a system designed to maintain a reciprocal balance among tribes. Widows of warriors had the right to demand the capture of men from other tribes to replace those lost, which in turn induced the other tribe to seek its own replacements. The result was a never-ending series of feuds and mutual abductions. The people who put forward Native Americans as models of reciprocity may not exactly have such intertribal arrangements in mind.

Perhaps the most terrifying example of what the bare search for a natural harmony, absent other considerations, can mean occurred among the Aztecs. Like other Mesoamerican high cultures (Olmecs, Toltecs, Mayas—and even the Incas in South America), the Aztecs thought that without blood offerings, the balance of nature would be upset and monstrous beings would emerge from the darkness to tear the cosmos apart. Jacques Soustelle, an admiring but honest historian of Aztec ritual, describes the special sacrifices required to keep the heavens revolving:

The astronomer priest made a sign: a prisoner was stretched out on the stone. With a dull sound the flint knife opened his chest

95

and in the gaping wound they spun the firestick, the *tlequauitl*. The miracle took place and the flame sprang up, born from this shattered breast; and amid shouts of joy messengers lit their torches at it and ran to carry the sacred fire to the four corners of the central valley. And so the world had escaped its end once more. But how heavy and blood-drenched a task it was for the priests and the warriors and the emperors, century after century to repel the unceasing onslaughts of the void.[10]

This too is harmony with nature, but a harmony that depends, as all such philosophical concepts do, on your beliefs about nature and the gods. Even the most ardent multiculturalist may pause in the face of such natural harmony and decide that there may be limits to modern pluralism and native wisdom after all.

Pre-Columbian Paradise?

A large body of archeological material has appeared recently that is gradually confuting idealistic attempts to portray ancient Native Americans as innocents living in harmony with nature. That idealism is most graphically represented in the peaceful and colorful murals of the Mexican artist Diego Rivera, which are enjoying a renewed appreciation as the anniversary of Columbus's first voyage approaches. Rivera's paintings show exactly the contours of the paradise many people would like to believe existed in pre-Columbian America: vistas of fertile plains spreading between breathtaking mountains; gaily dressed Indian peasants bending over neatly arranged plots of corn; community life steeped in the rhythm of the seasons, religious festivals, and songs. In short, an America before machines and automobiles, cities and suburbs, alleged alienation and cultural vacuity. While nostalgia for earlier, supposedly simpler times is a perennial theme of literature and art, rarely is the wish further from the reality than it is in Rivera's work. The murals may be pleasing art, but they are bad history.

The Nobel Prize–winning Mexican poet Octavio Paz has written several of the most lucid and accessible essays on pre-Columbian civilization in Mexico. These graceful commentaries combine both recent archeological and historical research with genuine affection for Mexico's dual heritage. Paz, in short, seems to have no particular axe to grind. The town he grew up in contained the usual seventeenth-century Spanish Baroque convents and nine-teenth-century buildings, but these stirred his imagination far less than the small Indian pyramid he and friends discovered while on a picnic one day. Both Mexico's Spanish and Indian heritage are deeply present in Paz's poetry, particularly in his *Piedra de sol*, a long poem based on the Mayan calendar.[11]

Paz has described the Mesoamerican Indian culture as a world of city-states perpetually at war with one another under the leadership of kings who proclaimed themselves divine. Kirkpatrick Sale may write glibly of a European culture of death, but some high Indian cultures, like the Aztecs and Mayas, were far more openly cults of blood and death than anything in the Old World. If the biblical religions are anti-natural, what of this:

> The religious foundation common to all the Mesoamerican peoples is a basic myth: the gods sacrificed themselves to create the world; the mission of the human being is to preserve the universal life, including his own, feeding the gods with the divine substance: blood. This myth explains the central place of sacrifice in Mesoamerican civilization. Thus, war is not only a political and economic dimension of the city-state but a religious dimension.[12]

One of the principal aims of war was to capture enemies alive who might be sacrificed later either on the altar or in a ritual ball game. Their hearts were cut out and offered to the gods of war and fertility.

As kinds of divinities themselves, the king and his queen were also expected to shed their own blood for cyclical renewal of the cosmos and the harvest. An elaborate system of rituals grew up in which the king practiced bloodletting on himself—among the Mayas this was often from his penis. The queen shed blood into a basin, usually from her tongue, which was pierced and a rope passed through it. Thus, through the repeated ritual offering of blood—both their own and others'—was the original energy of the cosmos restored and the end of the world postponed. The sheer quantity of blood needed was striking as well: tens of thousands were sacrificed, so far as we can tell, at great festivals and at the consecration of major temples from Mexico to Peru. Amid the changes in style and personalities over the centuries, the underlying cyclical pattern of cosmic order remained pretty much the same.

An odd double standard permeates much of the writing about these matters. For example, if the Spanish kings of the period had required human sacrifice to preserve their world and rule, as all evidence shows the Aztec and Mayan kings did, a modern hermeneutic of suspicion would unmask the ideology of death behind the religious veneer. But even useful and lucid historical accounts such as Davíd Carrasco's *Religions of Mesoamerica* highlight the astronomy, art, and other cultural achievements of native civilizations while treating the darker aspects as puzzling aberrations.[13] Carrasco goes so far as to rebuke the Spaniards, even the best of the missionaries, for thinking that they needed to convert the natives from their traditional religions. The Spaniards saw human beings dismembered, decapitated, and sacrificed amid sacred serpents. The priests performing the sacrifices were forbidden to cut their hair or nails, or wash the gore from their bodies—a horrifying image that does not appear on any wall painted by Diego Rivera. Recalling the abominations denounced in the Old Testament, the Spaniards concluded that the Indians were worshipping demons. Modern readers may judge what, under the circumstances, their own reactions might have been, and whether the most liberal among them would have felt obliged to respect Indian belief in the need to preserve natural cycles and harmony by such practices.

The Aztecs believed they were living in the era of the Fifth Sun and had very little sense of their own past or that of surrounding tribes. Mircea Eliade has shown with some force in *Cosmos and History* that this cyclic pattern, and rituals to preserve it, are common to most archaic societies.[14] Those of us who live in the "historical," linear time of the West, which is the direct result of the unfinished story of the Bible, have great difficulty believing that history proper does not exist among most other peoples. Chronicles record the cycles of creation-destruction-creation bound up with war and bloodshed, reality and myth, but there is no history proper, either in theory or in practical life. History as we know it combines the directional time of the Bible with a critical sifting of evidence begun by the ancient Greeks. Ironically, it is the putatively Eurocentric culture that has discovered much of Native American history—a fact of some importance if we wish to measure the effect of Europe on Native American self-understanding.

The Cost of Isolation

For Paz and other scholars isolation from outside influences not only created stagnant social forms in Mesoamerica but doomed the Native Americans whom the Spaniards encountered. In addition to their technical advantages in weaponry, the Spaniards had cultural advantages. European ignorance in the face of Indian culture, of which we hear so much today, was relatively small compared with Aztec ignorance about Europeans. While the Aztecs believed that these bearded men with six legs (i.e., mounted on horses) must be strange beings or gods, the Spaniards quickly obtained a general sense of the Indian religious, political, and social systems. Cortés immediately intuited how to use conquered tribes' resentment of Moctezuma's empire and how to appeal to human sentiments in his efforts to stop human sacrifice. At least for a time, Cortés and his men appeared to several subject peoples as liberators from political tyranny and from the burden of paying tribute to Indian rulers in human lives. In an odd, providential way, these highly unworthy Spanish vessels also became the bearers of a sort of liberation theology. Several thousand Indians joined the conquistadores in their assault on Mexico City.

By contrast, the Aztecs had no way of conceptualizing who or what the Spaniards were. As most readers of the early history of the Americas know, Moctezuma was terrified by an ancient prophecy that predicted the empire would be conquered by gods coming from where the sun rises. (By an odd historical coincidence it appears the prophecy also specified the exact year, *Ce Acatl* or 1-Reed, that the Spaniards landed on the Mexican coast, though later events may have contaminated the original accounts.) Aztec thought allowed only two categories of beings: gods and men. And the men were divided only between those belonging to their own sedentary civilization and those outside it, the barbarians. Because the Spaniards did not fit entirely into either category, the Native American tradition was of little help in confronting them.

Even before the arrival of Cortés, however, Indian culture had been crippled by a lack of contact with fresh influences. While Indian civilization produced some remarkable art and architecture over more than a millennium, no new impulses, such as had occurred elsewhere on the globe, led to the development of metals and the wheel, or to the breeding and training of animals for agricultural work. Whatever evils the Spaniards eventually introduced—and they were many and varied—they at least cracked the age-old shell of a culture admirable in many ways but also pervaded by repugnant atrocities and petrification. Anyone who wishes to defend the rights of surviving Indian tribes and to help preserve their cultures, two noble undertakings, must nevertheless be aware of what should and should not be retained from their heritage.[15]

Inevitable Tragedy

For Octavio Paz the encounter between the Old and New Worlds in his country led to fatal tragedy: "For two thousand years, the cultures of Mesoamerica lived and grew by themselves; their encounter with *the other* was too late and in conditions of a terrible inequality. For that reason, they were demolished."[16] We may regret much of what occurred, but we should recognize that it would have taken superhuman prescience and virtue on the part of the Spaniards to help the natives evolve peacefully toward a culture combining the best of both worlds. This did not happen in North or South America, in British India or French Vietnam. The encounter of two civilizations, especially when they are of widely differing cultural character, may involve more complexities than mere human intelligence and will can control.

The early record clearly shows as much. The most vivid eye-witness account of these first contacts on the American mainland is Bernal Diaz del Castillo's remarkably vigorous *Historia Verdadera de la Conquista de la Nueva España* (True History of the Conquest of New Spain). Diaz del Castillo was one of the conquistadores who came ashore with Cortés and is, therefore, viewed with suspicion by a certain type of historian. Why his narrative warrants more skepticism than any other history, however, is not clear. While Diaz del Castillo may not be a completely reliable source, he is far less biased than many of his detractors. He was moved to write initially, he says, by the false accounts of other early historians. Referring to one heroic chronicle of the conquest, written at a time when the numbers of Indians killed was regarded as a military achievement rather than an embarrassment, he remarks:

> When I had read it, I found that the whole was a misrepresentation, and also that in his extraordinary exaggerations of the numbers of the natives, and of those who were killed in the different battles, his account was utterly unworthy of belief. We never much exceeded four hundred men, and if we found such numbers bound hand and foot, we could not have put them to death.[17]

The simple but shrewd Diaz del Castillo tries, instead, to describe accurately what happened, as well as Cortés's real strengths and many weaknesses.

He also speaks credibly of the natives. Like many of his companions, Diaz del Castillo marvels at Aztec achievements and even regrets that, as he writes, many—particularly the stunning buildings of Tenochtitlán—had been destroyed. But as a faithful reporter, he paints less flattering pictures too. Even in the small villages the Spaniards enter, human sacrifice is widespread. When Cortés is offered gifts of friendship by one tribe, he asks sincerely that they first give up these sacrifices, which he regards as worshipping idols. Diaz del Castillo explains: "for every day our sight was offended by the repetition of four or five of these horrid murders, the unfortunate victims being cut up and their limbs sold in the public markets, as beef is in the towns of Old Castille."[18] Each time the Spaniards conquer a new town and the inhabitants flee, they come upon the blood and bones of young men recently sacrificed. Diaz del Castillo reports these discoveries with the same regularity and matter-of-fact tone as he uses to report on architecture, food, and weapons. The modern person who would try to judge fairly the actions of the conquistadores and the Indians must first appreciate how appalling these practices must have been to have repeatedly horrified even these battle-hardened soldiers.

North American Tribes

Writers about Native Americans farther to the north often try to distance those tribes from Mesoamerican cultures, or blame Aztec influence for unsavory practices north of the Rio Grande. The Pawnee, for example, are known to have sacrificed a young maiden yearly, but a typical explanation is that the ritual "may well have derived from a Mesoamerican culture more than a thousand miles to the south."[19] No evidence for this "may well have" is cited, or available. Despite its relative infrequency among North American tribes, human sacrifice is assumed to have been imported. It is said to have jumped to or been preserved by the Pawnee, but not originated by them. Even ethnology occasionally seems slanted against southern peoples and to favor northern groups.

In fact, North American tribes rivaled their Latin American counterparts in possessing all sorts of rituals and cultural practices that are incompatible with modern notions of civilized society. In the previous chapter we examined the shocking torture of captives by Iroquois, Algonquian, and northeastern tribes. Among the Plains Indians, Sioux men and women—the warm, gentle humanists in Kevin Costner's highly popular film *Dances With Wolves*—offered sacrifices of their own flesh during their yearly Sun Dance, which lasted several days and was the most common and typical Plains religious festival. Usually one man, seeking a vision from the sun god, volunteered to be hung up from skewers passed beneath his skin and tied to ropes (a ritual accurately portrayed in an older film, *A Man Called Horse*). Still others would subject themselves to slightly lesser torments while staring into the sun as long as they could bear.[20]

Each of these practices has an intelligible and purposive meaning within the Sioux system, and to describe them accurately should not be construed as an attempt to ridicule or discredit them. Rather, we need to become more fully aware of how profoundly *other* the beliefs and actions of Native American tribes really are. This crucial truth often escapes us when we are attracted to ways of life that seem to offer alternatives to the mechanical qualities and narrow rationality of modern life. People who would look askance at the ascetic practices of, say, Spanish Catholicism or English Puritanism, often remain blissfully ignorant of the actual religious beliefs and practices of the Native Americans they admire. But without a serious effort to understand these complex and deep spiritual concepts, we cannot possibly comprehend native relationships to the land and the relations among different tribes, let alone native life *per se*.

Unfortunately, at present, facile acceptance of all aspects of Native American religion seems to be the rule. At Princeton University the course on Native American religion has become the second most popular among undergraduates. Around 250 students enroll each semester. But David Carrasco, who teaches the course, has said that his greatest difficulty is getting students to be sufficiently critical in their approaches to the material.[21]

In this the undergraduates are simply following a broad cultural trend. New Age religious currents have appropriated—and grossly distorted—Indian beliefs. Because belief, ritual, and life-style are so inextricably intertwined in Native American cultures, authentic indigenous spirituality has been seriously neglected in this process, while exploiters and hucksters have profited.[22] The hope that Native Americans somehow possessed a lost and much-needed wisdom has been channeled into harmonic convergences, dial-an-Indian services, and sweat-lodge therapies. So common-place is this element of popular culture that the porno star-turned-performance artist and sex therapist Annie Sprinkle, who became famous when the National Endowment for the Arts denied her a grant, has blithely stated that her therapy includes "Native American techniques."[23]

Native American Feminism?

In a similar vein Native Americans have been enlisted among natural feminists and touted as worshippers of a primal mother goddess. But here, too, multicultural hopes may not be able to withstand historical reality. Bernal Diaz del Castillo reports, clearly with some titillation, on how batches of young women, some of them the nieces and daughters of Indian leaders, are presented to the conquistadores as gifts. Before accepting these ladies, the Spaniards usually require them to be baptized, a strange precondition, yet clearly not a mere formality. What stands out over and above the particulars of these exchanges, however, is the basic difference in attitude toward women. Contemporary political alliances grouping minorities and women cannot alter the fact that in pre-Columbian America women were sometimes op-pressed by the very groups we now regard as a minorities. While women occasionally occupied important posts in Aztec or other native societies, they were oftentimes treated like chattels. And though the Spaniards may have tolerated this practice for less-than-savory reasons, they certainly would not have been able to give away their own wives and daughters in Spain as gifts.

One of the facts most frequently cited by Columbus's critics in the current controversies is a passage from a letter written by his friend Michele de Cuneo:

> When I was in the boat I captured a very beautiful Carib woman, whom the said Lord Admiral gave to me, and with whom, having taken her into my cabin, she being naked according to their custom, I conceived desire to take pleasure. I wanted to put my desire into execution but she did not want it and treated me with her finger nails in such a manner that I wished I had never begun. But seeing that (to tell you the end of it all), I took a rope and thrashed her well, for which she raised such unheard of screams that you would not believe your ears. Finally we came to an agreement in such manner that I can tell you that she seemed to have been brought up in a school of harlots.[24]

If this is not a misrepresentation by Cuneo or a misleading account of what happened, Columbus surely deserves serious blame for subsequent Spanish mistreatment of native women.

Yet it is a crucial part of the historical picture to see clearly the status of women in parts of the pre-Columbian Caribbean. The Caribs, according to mainstream scholarship, not only were cannibals but made a habit of capturing women from the Arawak tribes—the peoples Columbus first encountered in the New World—and making them concubines. Women were segregated from the men to such an extent, moreover, that the two sexes spoke separate languages. Only the men spoke Carib; the women, even Carib women, spoke Arawak because of the large numbers of captive Arawak women among them.[25]

Nor were the Caribs an isolated instance of male domination in the New World. Modern Mexicans refer to Malinche, the Indian woman who served as Cortés's interpreter, as *la traidora* (the traitoress). Yet if we practice some feminist interpretation, her story may give us pause. A tribe allied with Aztecs sold her into slavery some years before the Spanish landed on the American mainland. (Native American tribes from the Southern Cone to Washington State practiced slavery, which poses another obstacle to modern multicultural alliances based on easy assumptions of innocence and guilt.) When the Spanish arrived, Malinche knew several Indian dialects and quickly mastered Castilian. It does not take a feminist hermeneutic to understand why this talented and independent woman may have felt less than full solidarity with the Aztec nobles when the conquistadores offered her a chance for liberation from their rule.

Well-defined gender roles were also common among the more simply organized North American tribes. Some ingenious recent scholarship has tried to show that, like good postmodernists, Indians either did not have our sense of the polarities of gender or that they recognized as many as six "genders."[26] Yet it cannot be denied that constant warfare encouraged a natural division of labor between domestic and hunter/warrior occupations. Women were often sexually free before marriage, but after became little more than domestic drudges. Matrilineal social arrangements existed in many tribes perhaps because of female dominance in the household and the need to keep track of descent where multiple wives and divorce were prevalent. While women in such societies sometimes had the power to choose which male would lead the tribe and could depose him for poor performance of duties, it was almost universally the men who made decisions, including the crucial decision to go to war.

The modern feminist agenda finds very little fertile soil in traditional Native American societies. Indeed, the position of women in the Americas prior to European contacts was generally worse than it was in the so-called European patriarchies. Nor do the hierarchies, castes, slavery, tribalism, and other evident features of various Native American societies support the conclusion that the New World provided a pristine alternative to the shortcomings of European societies. Though those societies are frequently lumped together as some evil monolith bearing down on native peoples, the Spanish, English, French, Dutch, and Portuguese who led the way to the New World actually represented a great multiplicity within a loose unity, which was Europe in 1492 and after.

Renaissance Europe

In the postcolonialist world in which we live, Europe's relation to the rest of the world is being recalibrated not only in the political realm but in intellectual history. Long-suppressed or absent voices of non-European peoples are rightly gaining a hearing. Frequently, these voices take on the tone of Caliban in Shakespeare's *The Tempest*, which is set, not incidentally, in the very Caribbean Columbus entered. In the postcolonial dispensation, Caliban now elicits more sympathy than he once did when he cries out:

> You taught me language, and my profit on't
> Is I know how to curse. The red plague rid you
> For learning me your language!
> (I.ii.366–68)

Changed historical circumstances have also brought about reevaluations of "civilization" and "barbarism," justice and rebellion.[27]

Curiously, America had a similar effect on Europe early in colonial history. Contemporary rereadings of history are the direct heirs of works like Thomas More's *Utopia*, in which the fictional source is one Raphael, who is presented as having traveled with Amerigo Vespucci during his voyages. Another character in that book laments: "I don't know whose fault it was, mine, yours, or Raphael's, but we never thought of asking, and he never thought of telling us whereabouts in the New World Utopia is."[28] Standing sufficiently far away in some vague location, Utopia—"No Place"—is able to serve as a blank slate on which to write a criticism of European society. More wrote almost a century before Shakespeare, but even in the early seventeenth century the New World remained for Europeans a useful *tabula rasa* for making seemingly objective comments that, in reality, were self-criticism. Renaissance Europe did not wait for the arrival of critics of Eurocentrism to begin feeling the effects of other peoples.

In many ways the new critique of Europe is desirable, when it is well informed, because it corrects an intellectual imperialism that Europe has exercised for too long over the histories of other peoples. But the sheer violence of the present pursuit of justice often causes such corrections to introduce new intellectual injustices, particularly in regard to the full record of European influence. The previous chapter traced some religious and secular currents within Europe that sought just action from the very beginnings of the European presence in the Americas. As Europe expanded into all parts of the globe, it brought domination, torture, death, and slavery of its own, but also bore other seeds that were to exert some crucial influence for the good.

The mixture of all the world's peoples, which is now our native condition, especially in the Americas, owes whatever success it has had not only to European exploration but to European pluralism. As the distinguished historian J. H. Elliott has observed:

> Divided into competing political units—and also, from the sixteenth century, into competing religious units—Renaissance Europe was a pluralist society, with none of the monolithic central control that characterized the contemporary Ottoman and Chinese empires. While having no doubt of the superiority of its own religion and way of life, it was less dismissive of the "barbarians" beyond its own borders than was the Chinese world.[29]

Elliott also cites as evidence of growing European universalism a principle that he found in the work of the theologian Francisco de Vitoria, who observed that the Indians' display of rationality had shown them to be "citizens of the whole world, which in a certain way constitutes a single republic."[30] Explorers' records, too, indicate a certain curiosity about and tolerance for the new peoples they discovered. Europe was neither the simple vehicle of enlightened civilization nor the bearer of monolithic imperialism to the rest of the world. We might do well to notice the evidence of openness within the vigorous expansion that is overlooked in generally heated postcolonialist debates.

Needy, Materialist Europe?

Opposed to this view of Europe, however, is a hard ideological stance that virtually identifies Europe with several burgeoning modern pathologies. The well-known portrait of late-medieval cruelty and suffering in Johan Huizinga's *The Waning of the Middle Ages* is often combined with Marxist, neo-Marxist, and radical environmentalist critiques of capitalist culture to produce a vivid picture of a morbid and rapacious European continent. Europe's relatively poor soil, limited landmass, and consequent famines supposedly drove its peoples into terrifying exploits. Kirkpatrick Sale, for example, turns Ferdinand Braudel's analyses of European economic woes and ambitions into an entire historiography. Sale sees a uniquely needy Europe pillaging other wealthy, abundant, sedentary civilizations. Quoting Braudel, he argues that "although other maritime cultures might have tried to compete on the seas, only Europe—mark the verb—'needed' the rest of the world, needed to venture outside its own front door."[31]

This characterization of an entire continent is, of course, absurd. Most "needs" stem from the indefinable combination of fantasy, enlightenment, enterprise, and curiosity that are inextricably part of the human person. Only a very few needs, such as shortages leading to starvation, can be measured in absolute terms. Famines have occurred in all parts of the world, and Europe is hardly unique in needing to remedy them. From what we know of tribal pressures and displacements among Eastern Woodland Indian tribes and Mesoamerican empires, Native Americans too were no strangers to need and conquest, nor were other indigenous peoples. What was unique about Europe, perhaps, was the belief that relatively long-distance, large-scale undertakings, necessitated by Europe's position as a rocky outcrop of coastline on the Asian landmass, was worth the effort.

Furthermore, those needs Europe did have for foreign goods did not quite result in the desperate quest that Sale's interpretation of Braudel suggests. Nowhere do the medieval and Renaissance courts of Europe give the impression of a feverish search for

109

sustenance in wealth or goods. Portugal and Spain, the two principal exploring nations at the start of the period, are quite measured in their decisions about what they will and will not undertake. The Portuguese voyages down the coast of Africa seem to be a sign of a swelling enthusiasm nurtured by Prince Henry the Navigator, but no mad rush for resources to save a sinking continent. Columbus's own experience with his patrons—their doubts about his "enterprise of the Indies," their long delays and deliberations, and their meager assignment of only three ships to such a task—indicates the Spanish crown's solid but circumspect interest in potential trade. Columbus personally, as we discussed in chapter two, was a unique blend of personal ambition and religious millenarism; thus his restlessness cannot be attributed to strict physical need.

Energetic Societies

Recent scholarship paints a far different picture of the sixteenth-century culture that was about to reshape the world. George Holmes, editor of the *Oxford Illustrated History of Medieval Europe,* remarks in the conclusion of that volume that

late Medieval Europe was certainly not a poor society. On the contrary we find evidence everywhere of high levels of income, greater sophistication in domestic comfort and artistic taste, and great vigour in both the economic and aesthetic spheres. Paradoxically it was a Europe reduced in population by the plagues but bursting with energetic life which began the conquest of the non-European world with the explorations of Vasco da Gama and Christopher Columbus.[32]

This is a far cry from the gloomy and frantic picture of a despairing 1492 Europe painted by the most radical revisionist critics.

The historian of late-medieval and Renaissance Europe John R. Hale has argued that Europe's lead in exploration arose not from weakness but strength, cultural as well as material:

In spite of privileges exercised by kings, feudal lords, priests and guilds, the individual's freedom of action was less circumscribed than in caste-divided India, or in family-centered China, or under the priest-kings of Central and South America. Moreover, in spite of plagues and local famines, the standard of living in Europe was higher than elsewhere. Revolutions are the work not of the cowed and starving, but of those who have enough to want more: Renaissance Europe, having recovered from the ravages of the terrible Black Death plague of the 14th Century, was sufficiently comfortably off to want to become rich.[33]

These factors, combined with some of the dynamic this-worldly elements in Christianity, says Hale, are what prodded Europe to do what no other high civilization of the time attempted. Confidence, not need or desperation, in part explains European exploration, which brought to the rest of the world more than mere reckless flailings.

A certain worldly restlessness and sense of superiority showed itself in the Europe of this period. But neither of these characteristics is purely a fault. Hale points to the "almost senile complacency" of China at the time, whose earlier exploration in the Indian Ocean was hardly even exploration. The Chinese loaded seventeen thousand soldiers and great displays of wealth onto large fleets and expected that the inferior peoples, seeing these manifestations of Chinese culture and power, would simply desire to join themselves to the Celestial Empire. Facing this flotilla, heads of state understandably agreed to go to China and do homage to the emperor. Whatever faults Christian Europe manifested in its explorations of the world, it showed more humility than that. Europeans at least believed that they had to exert themselves to gain new resources and win over converts to their ways. Compared with the Chinese sense of superiority, European self-assertion was modesty itself.

Most critics of Eurocentrism have failed to notice another crucial fact. Unlike cultures as diverse as the Aztecs in Tenochtitlán and the Imperial Court in Peking, Europe in the age of exploration did not consider itself the center of the world. On European maps of the time, Jerusalem is both the spiritual and geographic center of the earth. A determined anti-Eurocentrist might make the case that this is merely a mask for imperialism. Nevertheless, it demonstrates in concrete terms what principles dominated even conceptions of the globe—religious principles, not nationalist or economic ones.

Ultimately, how we judge Europe's energy since 1492 depends on whether we think certain human developments over the last five hundred years were or were not good. Machiavelli, for example, saw in the tensions and conflicts among Italian city-states the very wellsprings of political vitality in early-sixteenth-century Italy.[34] These oppositions were to a great extent mirrored in complex European currents that help explain both that continent's turmoil and its vitality.

The Rigors of Modernity

Another major critique of Renaissance Europe charges that its complexity demonstrates a fragmentation caused by growing capitalism and materialism. Kirkpatrick Sale goes so far as to observe that "not for nothing is this the age that invents polyphony and counterpoint in music and double-entry bookkeeping in commerce, that knew such a babel of vernacular languages that Leonardo da Vinci at the time feared 'the generation of man will come to pass as not to understand each other's speech.' "[35] Paradoxically, though, the same writer criticizes Spain—and the other budding nation-states—for incipient centralization of power and notes the sinister implications of Elio Antonio de Nebrija's compilation of the first Spanish grammar. When questioned by Queen Isabella about what use such a book might have, de Nebrija reportedly answered, "Language has always been the companion of Empire."[36] For some critics, then, Europe was both falling apart in dangerous fashion and consolidating power in dangerous fashion. But whether it was coming to speak too many languages or too few, it was embarking on a mission that would transmit all future evils to the rest of the world.

112

Just one indication of how simple-minded such assertions are may be glimpsed in the use Native Americans made of Spanish in the New World. Sam Gill, a brilliant student of Native American religion, remarks:

> During the seventeenth century, Spanish had become well established as a second language, providing a lingua franca among the many native peoples whose languages were unintelligible to one another; yet they retained their own languages and even made efforts to keep them free of Spanish words. Spanish became an instrument used by the Pueblo peoples against Spanish intrusions, in that it permitted them to better communicate among themselves. It helped support the growing sense of unity and common identity that replaced the antagonisms that existed prior to Spanish contact.[37]

This linguistic phenomenon reflects, perhaps better than anything else, the condition that Europe had uniquely experienced within itself and was to bequeath, despite atrocities and imperialism, to the rest of the world: a new dynamic of particularity within unity.

It is inevitable that the most influential culture in the past half millennium should receive the brunt of the blame for the world's evils. Oddly, however, it receives none of the credit for the good. The complexity of European society makes simple attribution of one trait to it without other contradictory or counterbalancing traits next to impossible. Papal power, for example, carried with it certain negative traits. But in Renaissance Europe, as in formerly Communist modern Eastern Europe, a universal moral and spiritual authority was sometimes useful against local state powers, whatever problems of its own it may have generated.[38] As we have seen in the previous chapter, independent moral authority played no small role in taming the worst abuses in Spanish America.

Of course, the radical critique of the Europe of the last five hundred years contains many important truths. It often recapitulates the old European philosophical debate between the ancients and the moderns. To oversimplify somewhat, the ancients (including Jews and Christians) believed in a cosmos created and ordered by a divine principle that made it possible to identify correct personal and social modes of behavior. The Ten Commandments, the Christian appropriation of Aristotle, and the Stoic tradition of the virtues, among many other manifestations of Western thought, show a common belief in the order and limits of nature. The Enlightenment, scientific revolution, Industrial Revolution, modernism, and postmodernism all, to one degree or another, abandon that view for the more rationalist position that human intelligence can and should be applied to nature to "relieve man's estate," in Francis Bacon's famous phrase.[39] The success of science—and the crisis in values attending that success—is the warp and woof of much current philosophical inquiry.

Today, while we generally feel that our scientific and technological capacity is adequate for most purposes, we worry about the environmental damage and human aridity that seem to be unfortunate by-products of our material success. Anxiety about our own state makes us susceptible to claims about pre-modern societies, particularly little-known, non-Western ones. Few people would wish to return to medieval European society, a telling reluctance. For there is a vast price to pay for jettisoning the moderns wholesale. While we may desire to minimize the effects of industry on the environment and even to resacralize nature and culture, there is no simple return for us to pre-modern religious and philosophical traditions—whether from Europe or from non-Western cultures whose entire conceptual framework would quickly lead to the abandonment of modern modes of agriculture and the death by starvation of hundreds of millions of people.

Turning our backs on all of the modern tradition would also involve intellectual regressions. Many people blame medieval Europe or Puritan New England for the persecution of witches, for example, but witches were a common fear among Eastern Woodland and other Indian cultures as well. The Senecas believed in a kind of Manichaeism in which a good creator brother and a bad destroyer brother fight over the world. The False Face societies encountered by the early North American settlers performed "all sorts of acts on the model of the Bad Spirit . . . in order to cure disease, fight witchcraft, and remove disorder."[40] Unfortunately, our attraction to some Native American concepts of order and harmony does not allow us to select them at will from less-congenial beliefs—like the belief in witches. Native cultures were all of one piece. At this late date we can hardly accept fighting disease and other evils with magic.

European Intellectual Contributions

Interesting questions arise from the debate that has erupted over the use of the term "discovery" to describe what happened in 1492. Native peoples, argue those who object to the term, already knew who and where they were and did not need to be "discovered." While this is true in a sense, it is also false in crucial respects. The Mexican historian Edmundo O'Gorman has shown that for Europeans America was not discovered but invented.[41] The ancient and medieval European conception of a single land-mass encompassing Europe, Asia, and Africa had to give way to the empirical evidence provided by the voyages of exploration before the idea of America could come into being. Until then, probably sometime after Columbus's death in 1506, Europe was only adding data to its existing structure of beliefs about the world, not undergoing a revolution in geographical, philosophical, and even theological thought.

And across the Atlantic, Native American thought also had to undergo a revolution before being able to understand the true place of America in the world. Indians did *not* know who and where they were in important ways because they knew "the other" even less than did late-medieval Europeans. This is reflected in the difficulties we still have in naming the peoples inhabiting the New World in Columbus's time and their modern descendants. For most purposes "Native Americans" seems to have displaced "Indians" as a socially accepted term. Indians was the name Columbus gave to the peoples he thought were in the Indies. Columbus never knew that he had discovered America, nor was he to his dying day sure exactly what he had found on his voyages.

Terminology, as Native American leaders have emphasized, is

115

not neutral in sorting out historical issues. But the questions are more complex than those leaders usually admit. Native American, too, is a less-than-perfect, even misleading term, and not only because it invites confusion with all other people born and raised in the United States. "America" was named after Columbus's contemporary, the Florentine Amerigo Vespucci, and Native American suggests that the various peoples in these lands were all part of one easily identifiable cultural or racial entity—defined in European terms. For the indigenous peoples themselves had no term for this diverse group and were not even aware of themselves and their land as constituting two of the continents of the world. That realization came much later and only in response to the European presence.

While it is probably fair to deny that Columbus "discovered" America, it would be unfair to ignore the fact that he did something more far-reaching. He may not have proved the world was round for Europeans, but he did for Native Americans. And in so doing, he inaugurated the age in which, finally, all the world's people inhabited one world *and knew they inhabited it*, though that realization was slow to be accepted in many newly discovered lands. Europe does not have the right to define the history of non-European peoples, but—by virtue of its geographical and intellectual contributions—European thought necessarily became the framework within which even non-European histories would henceforth have to be worked out. Moreover, given Europe's pluralism—its distinctive multiplicity within a kind of unity that was, after a long struggle, to lead to recognition of universal rights and their embodiment in law—the multiculturalist effort to destroy Eurocentric thought is doomed at the outset. The wish to contest an allegedly monolithic European view of history with fresh voices and perspectives inescapably belongs to a very European mode of thought.

A Concluding Parable

Let us conclude with a parable:
In 1638 the French explorer and interpreter Jean Nicollet be-

lieved he might have finally discovered the water route to Cathay. Nicollet had "gone native," living for many years among the Algonquins of Allumette Island and the Nipissings, and becoming conversant with their cultures and languages. He returned to the French settlement at Three Rivers on the Saint Lawrence because he remained a convinced Catholic and apparently did not wish to live without the sacraments.[42] A better early exponent of multiculturalism would be hard to come by in North America.

The Nipissings circulated stories that hairless people from far away were trading beyond the Great Lakes to the west. Since the time of Marco Polo, such anecdotes suggested to Europeans Chinese or Japanese dignitaries. Nicollet set out to find these people, having taken care to bring with him an embroidered robe of Chinese damask. When he landed on the western shore of Lake Michigan, he put on the robe and, holding a pistol in each hand, cut quite a figure as he marched into the village of Winnebago Indians at what is now Green Bay, Wisconsin. After three days of exploring, he was sure from native accounts that only three days distant was the "great water" to Cathay. The Indians meant the Mississippi.

Multiculturalists who seek some transcendent deliverance in the American wilderness resemble Nicollet. However much they know about Native American and Western cultures (usually little, and probably far less than Nicollet), their quest is driven primarily by deep currents within the now-global culture inspired by Europe. The quest is not wholly misguided. After all, Cathay exists, as do solutions to many current Western problems. But to solve the problems, as to reach Cathay, requires true knowledge and a broader perspective than that provided by the most typical forms of multiculturalism. The Celestial Kingdom was not, and is not, in the Americas.

5

Events and Counter-Events

> We understand the official celebration of the quincentenary
> (and its commercial variants) as an imperial liturgy not
> only retelling lies of the past, but building a consensus for
> more of the same: a two-tiered system of global and
> domestic economic apartheid.
> — 1992/Kairos USA[1]

On October 12, 1992, along the coast of the island of San Salvador, where Columbus is believed to have made first landfall in the Americas, the sun will rise on a strange ceremony. A group of ecologists will conduct a funeral service for "the natural environment of the Western Hemisphere" and mourn the destruction of native peoples and species that has occurred since 1492. While this event probably reaches a high-water mark for New Age daffiness over the quincentenary, it is by no means uncharacteristic of the kinds of public events that will have marked 1992. In fact, far from being an eccentric and countercultural act, the proposed funeral service has received sympathetic treatment and advance publicity in one of the central documents issued by the U.S. government's Smithsonian Institution in anticipation of the Columbus commemorations.[2]

In the United States, environmentalism will drive much of the large-scale negative reactions to the quincentenary. While the public has sympathy for the plight of surviving Native Americans and dislikes residual racial prejudice against African-Americans, neither of these issues—anymore than real or imagined injustices

119

by European settlers—is strong enough by itself to galvanize public opinion. The environment, however, touches everyone, and appeals to environmental worries have helped gain general acceptance for more radical critiques. Winona LaDuke, a well-known Native American and feminist activist who speaks frequently on college campuses, explained as much in the radical evangelical magazine *Sojourners*:

> The ecological agenda is what many indigenous people believe can, and must, unite all peoples in 1992. That agenda calls for everyone to take aggressive action to stop the destruction of the Earth, essentially to end the biological, technological, and ecological invasion/conquest that began with Columbus's ill-fated voyage 500 years ago.[3]

Official Views

Such apocalyptic views are not confined to a small and embattled minority. As we have seen in chapter one, the most extensive and sober government-sponsored events commemorating 1492 betray similar impulses. For example, the Smithsonian's primary quincentenary exhibition, "Seeds of Change," which for the most part restricts itself to recording the human and environmental effects, good and bad, produced by the mixture of New and Old Worlds, also sounds an ominous warning. In the book accompanying the exhibit, Frank H. Talbot, the director of the National Museum of Natural History, expresses the hope that it will "encourage the urgently needed redefinition of our relationship with our world and its peoples."[4]

Herman J. Viola, co-editor of the book and director of the quincentenary programs at the museum, explains the vision behind that aim. Viola is a generally sound scholar (his book *After Columbus: The Smithsonian Chronicle of the North American Indians* is a useful guide to Native American history), but he tends to make extreme statements when he focuses on some issues. About the environment, for instance, he claims: "What had taken nature thousands of centuries to create was largely undone in less than

120

five, beginning in September 1493, when the Admiral of the Ocean Sea returned to America at the head of an armada of seventeen ships."[5] Even those of us deeply concerned about environmental damage may hesitate to describe the past five hundred years as having "largely undone" nature. Though this may be only a slip, it is a telling one from the director of such a prestigious public event.

The bulk of the exhibit is devoted to clear, well-documented explanations of changes around the world generated by Europe's first contacts with the Americas. Corn, tomatoes, potatoes, peppers, peanuts, yams, turkeys, and various other foods were indigenous to the Americas. Their introduction to Europe, Africa, and Asia altered eating patterns, politics, and culture. Corn provided additional calories for people and livestock in Africa, and both corn and potatoes helped Europe feed itself more easily. Potatoes grew well even in northern Europe's rocky soil and could be left in the fields until needed, enabling the northern nations to become stronger and challenge the traditionally dominant countries of southern Europe. The slowly improving diet of the European nations in general, it is believed, helped them become more populous and more assertive around the globe. In a paradoxical way, then, America's crops fed European imperialism.

Similarly, introduction of European animals and plants reshaped the Americas. Wheat, apples, and grapes have certainly flourished here; pigs and horses, which had become extinct in the hemisphere after the last Ice Age, were reintroduced by the Europeans and changed the culture of the Plains Indians and other tribes for good. We now find it hard even to imagine the Plains Indians without the horses that they integrated so majestically into their traditional culture. Sugarcane brought to the Caribbean also increased the need for Africans to work the fields there because they were resistant to European and African diseases, as the natives of the Caribbean were not. So sweeteners and slavery fed one another.

This information, and much more of sound historical value to all America's ethnic groups, is registered in the exhibit. (The taped guide with the English-accented voice the Smithsonian favors for august occasions, however, pays Hispanics little respect by his repeated insistence that "con-kwist-a-dor" is the proper Spanish pronunciation of the term for Cortés and his men.) What is problematic about the show is the frame into which this picture is set—the introduction by Talbot and Viola, and the even-more-dubious concluding chapter by radical ecologists Steven King and Liliana Campos Dudley. The latter pair endorse not only the San Salvador funeral service for nature but a wide spectrum of environmentalist political nostrums of doubtful credibility. They all but canonize Chico Mendes, a Brazilian environmentalist murdered by Brazilian developers. Mendes may have been pursuing good aims and was brutally slain, but, as a member of the Brazilian Communist Party and a committed revolutionary (his son was named for the Sandinistas in Nicaragua and his daughter for a Brazilian terrorist), he carries other baggage along with him. Though these facts are well known, none is mentioned in the Smithsonian volume.[6] That the conclusion to a U.S. government–sponsored publication uses such materials uncritically indicates just how pervasive the radical environmentalist agenda has become. Indeed, official America shows little inclination to celebrate imperial liturgies in memory of 1492.

The Art World and 1492

Indisputable facts at least anchor most natural history. The officially sponsored artistic displays, however, have not been nearly as securely tied to historical reality. The other major government-supported exhibit, "Circa 1492: Art in the Age of Exploration," which had a brief run in the fall of 1991 at Washington's National Gallery of Art, seemed allergic to aligning itself in any way with the historical facts surrounding Columbus. As the exhibit catalog made clear, the show was "not about a man called Columbus. . . . [but] about the extraordinary age in which he played a part."[7] "Circa 1492" simply assembled quite striking works from several cultures directly involved or—in the case of Japan, China, and

India—that would have been involved in the upheavals of 1492 had Columbus arrived at his intended destination.

The problem with such an approach is its burial of the truly significant historical event that gives meaning to the exhibit beneath a falsely distorting and multiculturally neutral "Age of Exploration." And yet despite the enormous number of works he gathered together from different cultures, Jay A. Levenson, the managing curator and editor of the exhibit catalog, still feared sinning against the principle of equal representation:

> A survey that included, in acceptable depth, every significant culture that existed in the world of 1492 would be beyond the scope of any exhibition or catalogue. Difficult choices had to be made in each of the major sections of the show, and if a particular culture is not represented, that is likely to be because it is less central to the theme of that segment of the exhibition rather than because of any shortcomings in its artistic creations.

To mollify the excluded, Levenson poured out further multicultural libations:

> We have specifically tried to present each civilization on its own terms, not as it might have appeared to visiting Europeans of the period. . . . Homogeneity was not a feature of the world of 1492, and under no circumstances could a single theme have done justice to the amazing variety that characterizes the cultures that are represented in the show.[8]

The lesson of all this, of course, is that we have much to learn from the diversity and mutual interchanges of that period.

Unfortunately, to avoid privileging even this European perspective, the curator presents the lesson so indirectly that the entire exhibit illuminates neither art nor history. Instead, it vaunts hundreds of objects thought to illustrate a general social or political thesis. "Object" is the appropriate term here. Aztec ceremonial knives or Taíno throat ticklers used to induce vomiting in ritual purifications, for example, are not strictly speaking *objets d'art*. The historian Simon Schama wrote of this incoherent assemblage:

123

These problems of selection and scale are only symptoms of a deeper failure to understand what it means to historicize. Columbus's conspicuous banishment from the exhibition exemplifies the kind of approach that is willing to sacrifice the considerations of historical agency to a kind of milquetoast universalism. The mere presentation of contemporaneity, after all, explains nothing. Instead, the whole invidious, conflict-ridden mess of history disappears within the embrace of synchronicity. In the weightless historical space called "Circa 1492" no particular persons or powers actually bring about events. Indeed, there are no events; there are only phenomena hazily defined, formed and reformed and deformed with the shifting winds and tides of the zeitgeist, now medieval, now renaissance, now scientific-empirical-capitalist.[9]

This weightlessness and the refusal to allow any potentially controversial history to peak through the multicultural facade, Schama laments, characterizes "histories that are consciously designed as reparation."

Official Wariness

For the quincentenary, then, the two major public displays mounted by America's official cultural and historical institutions were far less an imperial liturgy and far more the kind of revision-cum-reparation favored by the critics of Columbus and his legacy. In fact, other than a brief remark during a Public Broadcasting Service (PBS) television special in which the mayor of Columbus, Ohio, said the admiral symbolized all that was good and decent and honest about the United States, it would be difficult to find an official statement unambiguously praising Columbus in the entire country.

In the late 1980s the U.S. government did set up a Christopher Columbus Quincentenary Jubilee Committee that was to plan somewhat traditional celebrations and events for 1992. But the whole enterprise soon ran aground. John N. Goudie, a Cuban native and Miami real-estate broker appointed by Ronald Reagan

124

to begin the preparations, became embroiled in shady financial dealings and eventually was questioned by the Congressional Subcommittee on Finances. Goudie contended that much of the two million dollars originally given to him (a small sum to be supplemented by private contributions) had been badly spent because of his ignorance of how the government works rather than through malfeasance. Nevertheless, he prudently invoked the Fifth Amendment thirty-two times during his Congressional testimony.[10]

But even without the mishandling of funds, it is doubtful that Goudie would have promoted a general celebration of Columbus. Garry Wills interviewed him before the controversies and found him chary of using the term "discovery" and pliant to outside pressures: "Russell Means complained about the word jubilee," Goudie said, "but I told him it is the Jewish word for a time of remembrance when one can redress wrongs."[11] Whether a jubilee under Goudie actually would have satisfied Means or other radical critics of Columbus is impossible to know. The financial mismanagement and Goudie's removal as the committee's head created such turmoil that the program was vastly reduced and weakly implemented.

On the more scholarly side of government activity, the Library of Congress under the leadership of James H. Billington published a well-written and thoroughly researched guide, *Keys to the Encounter*.[12] Though the text strives to avoid what its author, Louis De Vorsey, Jr., eccentrically calls a Europocentric view, it effectively points curious readers toward solid historical investigation and the wealth of source materials available at the Library of Congress. As Billington rightly emphasizes, encounters between civilizations cannot be understood without encounters between researchers and sources: "the knowledge therein can only be mined when someone actively seeks it out."[13] This obvious truism was worth repeating when so much about 1492 and after has come to be assumed.

The Organization of American States (OAS), the heirs of the Spanish and indigenous civilizations that created the New World,

125

also planned some quincentenary activities, but of a very cautious and low-key nature. For the most part the OAS was content to record the events and controversies within various member states. But such direction as the organization's efforts took may be gauged from a summary remark made by James Kiernan, the head of the OAS quincentenary programs: "Columbus sailed to find the Indies and started a process that was more catastrophic than the separation of the continents in the Pleistocene age."[14] Clearly, the OAS had no intention of sponsoring any forthright celebrations of Columbus.

Television Histories

One of the few serious public attempts to analyze the Columbus history emerged from a collaboration between the PBS and the National Endowment for the Humanities (NEH). Previous projects jointly undertaken by these two semi-independent government agencies have not always had happy results. Even under the chairmanship of William Bennett, a Reagan appointee and strong conservative, NEH had funded some wildly propagandistic leftist specials during the 1980s. "The Africans" drew particular ire for its one-sided history, and not only from conservatives. But the PBS-NEH "In Search of Columbus" arrived at a fairly straightforward presentation of its material, which was skewed only slightly to avoid overly controversial topics and to make some ritualistic bows to several contemporary constituencies.

Perhaps the main reason for the project's overall success was the choice of Mauricio Obregon, a longtime Columbus scholar and collaborator with Samuel Eliot Morison, as the principal researcher and narrator. Obregon is too serious a historian and too forceful a personality to have any simple readings of Columbus thrust upon him. He lucidly describes Europe in the fifteenth century and Europe's relations with other civilizations. If the seven-hour series tacitly settles many questions about Columbus that might be regarded as forever beyond our knowing, the argument at least never contradicts the evidence. Obregon's sheer enthusiasm for the subject and his meticulous research carry the storyline into interesting shoals and estuaries that more partisan approaches overlook.

Obregon traces, for example, the importance of trade for Islam, both as an economic activity and as a vehicle for Muslim evangelization. Mohammed himself, he reminds us, was a trader. Viewed against this Islamic background, Europe's search for new markets and new converts does not appear as unusually sinister in the world or as much a precursor of modern capitalism as some critics believe. We also get a glimpse into the psychology of trade in the period. Like Columbus, the Muslim traders were very secretive about their sources of supply. Information of this sort was worth a great deal of money. The Muslims were crafty enough, for instance, to keep secret the locations of the only two islands on earth where cloves could be found—cloves being worth their weight in silver at the time.

We also tour other civilizations of the late fifteenth century. China, after a brief burst of exploration to determine if any serious enemies might attack from the sea, decided the answer was no and settled into a self-satisfied isolation. Japan, one of Columbus's destinations, was so wealthy and sophisticated that a shogun around the time of Columbus's first voyage was able to build a temple decorated completely with gold leaf, the famous Golden Temple of Kyoto. African kingdoms the Europeans contacted also come into sharper focus. Before the arrival of the Europeans, the Ashanti in West Africa had already created extensive gold mines and were trading in slaves from the interior without moral scruple. Both these factors influenced European attitudes toward native peoples and the Africans themselves in the coming decades: wealth could be gotten from these contacts without too much delicacy about the human means used to extract it.

In sum, the series accurately reflects the qualities—positive, negative, and ambiguous—of the world's various societies in 1492. In his treatment of Columbus *per se*, however, Obregon wavers. He brings to the story many fine touches and beautiful photography, but like many other more-or-less official commentators, he avoids facing the toughest issues head on. The failed settlement at La Navidad and Columbus's subsequent harshness to rebellious natives and Spaniards, as well as his loyalty and continuing kindness to Guacanagarí, are quickly passed over. The viewer is left somewhat confused, therefore, when Obregon tells him in the final segment that Columbus "failed miserably as a governor." The encounter's potential for good and the roots of very definite evils are obscured by what can only be squeamishness about provoking controversy.

Also, Obregon often permits a multicultural din to drown out important observations. He is clear that, although the diseases introduced into the New World produced "perhaps the greatest human disaster of all time, it is one that no one—not even Christopher Columbus—can be faulted for." Even on the subject of well-known Spanish atrocities, Obregon draws together some useful judgments. He speaks of the "long and distinguished history of sword and cross being opposed," and has the eminent historian of the Spanish Empire J. H. Elliott explain how remarkable it was in history that the Spanish were "the first to denounce atrocities by their own compatriots." He also gives the Spanish New Laws of 1542 that outlawed slavery and limited the *encomienda* their proper due.

Unfortunately, the force of all this is diminished by other voices, which generally come from indigenous and African-American protesters. And while the opinions of these spokesmen are certainly understandable, they are not always firmly grounded in history or even very widely held by the people the leaders claim to speak for. Surveys taken of native populations in Latin America have shown a more mixed picture. Large majorities of Indians are grateful for the arrival of Christianity and European culture, though there is some regret over what was lost. The situation in Latin America, of course, differs from that in the United States where tribes were almost obliterated. In Latin America the indigenous peoples melded with Spaniards, and the series shows quite well how, in culture, religion, and racial features, a country like Mexico truly became a new nation, fusing new and old.

The dissenting voices, however, are simply allowed to accumulate in the series' final episode, which weighs the overall merits and defects of the encounter. Only after those protests have been heard does Obregon himself step forward and announce what is perhaps a courageous position under the circumstances. He concludes that we should not only remember or commemorate Columbus but actually *celebrate* the man who boldly inaugurated the new age in human history.

"The Buried Mirror"

"The Buried Mirror: Reflections on Spain and the New World," a Discovery Channel television series sponsored by the Smithsonian Institution, in part, and the Spanish Quinto Centenario España Foundation, also takes a basically evenhanded approach to the history of the Americas. Hosted by Mexican novelist Carlos Fuentes, it provides a remarkably balanced account of how two civilizations coalesced into one new civilization across vast religious, cultural, and material divides. Fuentes, who has made a career of denouncing U.S. imperialism while being lavishly supported as a visiting scholar at various U.S. universities, nevertheless manages in this instance to tell us of the good and bad on all sides.

Like his fellow Mexican Octavio Paz, Fuentes admires native cultures but does not indulge in non-historical idealizations. The fabulous remains of high civilizations in the Americas impress him with their serenity and sheer scale. For him such achievements exist on a plane comparable to that of ancient Mesopotamia or Egypt. While most of these Mesoamerican civilizations disappeared or regressed long before Columbus, Fuentes argues that their collective history—like the mirrors found beneath the earth at some Mayan archeological sites—help us to see some of our own features.

European and native civilizations present both parallels and contrasts. Spain hacked an empire out of the Americas with gunpowder and the sword, but the Aztecs and Incas had created

129

empires as well with the weapons available to them. The Aztecs used "tyranny, tribute, fear, and *la guerra florida* [the flowery war]" to gain the endless supply of prisoners they needed for human sacrifice. Fuentes goes so far as to characterize the Aztec gods as "a whole pantheon of fear," spiritual forces to be appeased or employed to combat threats posed by nature.

The difference between Moctezuma and Cortés is that the former was ruled by fate, the latter by will. Perfectly illustrating Machiavelli's conception of *virtú*, Cortés was able to make use of good fortune in his conquests. By contrast, Moctezuma was virtually helpless in the face of the strange new onslaught. For Fuentes, the conquistador's child by his interpreter and mistress La Malinche—a child who was the first *mestizo* on the mainland and therefore the first Mexican—symbolized the beginning of a truly new civilization. After that birth, fate and will, resignation and vigorous action, would be interwoven in the fabric of Mexican culture.

In the Spanish conquest of the Incas in Peru, Fuentes discerns a similar process at work amid the dirty business of politics and strife. By taking advantage of a civil war then going on between the sons of a recently dead Incan emperor, the unscrupulous adventurer Pizarro was able to conquer and impose his rule with only 180 Spanish soldiers. The Incan emperor was considered a god, the descendant of the sun. When that god was killed by Spaniards, the stage was set for a new empire to rise on the foundations of the old.

Fuentes returns often to Spain's constant examination of the moral questions connected with the conflict. Though he recognizes that this did not prevent the worst atrocities, he is right to point out that similar scruples never troubled the minds of other colonizing nations. About Christianity in particular, he makes a remarkable observation. Missionaries believed they had the right to convert Indians, he says, and a majority of them accepted the *encomienda* and other Spanish coercions as prerequisites to proper evangelization. Nevertheless, he notes an epochal shift in native cultures owing to Christian influence:

130

One can only imagine the astonishment of the hundreds and thousands of Indians who asked for baptism as they came to realize that they were being asked to adore a god who sacrificed himself for men instead of asking men to sacrifice themselves to gods, as the Aztec religion demanded.

Such positive developments are often overlooked out of deference and sensitivity toward surviving Indian communities.

Fuentes himself, in spite of the overall fairness he brings to the material, glosses over a problem after this observation. Showing Indians who currently practice a syncretism of Christianity and worship of old indigenous gods, as many continue to do, he repeats the often-enunciated plea that Indians are asking us only to "respect their values." It is, of course, a good thing to respect one another's values when those values are worth respecting, but such pieties run up against some hard facts. We certainly cannot respect ancient Indian ways in their entirety because, like European cultures, they contained some horrible things. And even existing practices may give us pause. People who point to Indian values as a remedy for our evil exploitation of the natural world are often squeamish about inhumane treatment of animals. How many of them, then, would feel comfortable watching the Indian rite— filmed by Fuentes's crew—of cutting the throats of young animals and sprinkling the blood libation collected in basins on the lintels of mines and houses? Here, as elsewhere, "respecters" of native cultures choose to emphasize elements from them that already have some standing in the mainstream culture.

Fuentes is guilty of worse lapses. After masterfully explaining some stone carvings and statues from Aztec times, he commits the error of aestheticizing them. Depictions of horrifying deities and terrible events, he says, no longer have religious meaning for us, and therefore we can regard them as striking art objects. This approach may calm the consciences of people who like Aztec "art" but who do not wish to take the trouble to learn about the ancient cultures. Perhaps it even accounts for much of modern aesthetic fascination with the primitive. But for anyone who thinks art has an intimate and dynamic connection to life, ignoring

1492 AND ALL THAT

the conceptual dimension of Aztec "art" is tantamount to ignoring the Napoleonic invasion of Spain when we look at Goya's *Desastres de la guerra* or forgetting Hitler's Luftwaffe when we see Picasso's *Guernica*. Fuentes himself is quick to mention the social contexts when he comments later on the two European works. The different approach to native objects not only willfully diminishes them as human creations, it falsifies the nature of the work itself.

Despite these lapses, however, Fuentes, created an informative, affectionate, and well-proportioned survey of American and European history and future prospects. Anyone who would see in the work of the longtime leftist Fuentes, or in that of the Columbus scholar Mauricio Obregon, an imperial liturgy must contemplate history through very thick ideological lenses indeed.

Lighter Fare

The only other major government-sanctioned public acknowledgment of the quincentenary was a special issue of *Newsweek* produced in conjunction with the "Seeds of Change" exhibit. Probably because the journalists who did most of the writing are not very inclined to accept romantic pieties from any quarter, the overall outline of events in those pages is extremely well balanced, despite its popular nature. The issue concludes with Raymond Sokolov, a former food critic for the *New York Times*, asking us to celebrate the culinary consequences of 1492. Putting aside the cultural anxiety over the quincentennial, Sokolov notes that all of us—Europeans and Asians, Africans and Native Americans—eat far better today because the globe has been united. The Chinese have made good use of hot peppers and peanuts; Europeans have grown fond of them, too, along with tomatoes, corn, and potatoes; and Native Americans now enjoy chicken, pork, beef, wheat, and various delicacies. In his book on the subject, Sokolov decided to observe a "Kirkpatrick Sale Day" by experimenting with pre-1492 menus of both Europe and the Americas—unappetizing concoctions like dry bread crusts and pond-scum cheeses—and demonstrated how much better it is today to savor the "progressive dinner in which the whole human race takes part but no one need leave home to sample all the courses."[15] In *Newsweek* he suggests we stop criticizing Columbus: "He is only a convenient scapegoat for our own self-hate and our own very modern doubts about the value of our culture. We and Columbus may have a lot to apologize for, but we also deserve plenty of credit."[16]

Oddly, *Newsweek*'s special issue conveys information much more effectively than does the contemporaneous October 1991 *National Geographic* entitled "1491: America Before Columbus." While the articles in this special supplement do show aspects of life in North America before the arrival of the Europeans, they focus on only a small portion of that life. Clearly, several dozen pages could not do justice to the hundreds of American Indian tribes, but the inadequacies are more fundamental than that. What is covered is reduced to *National Geographic*'s usual categories of the visually beautiful and the alluringly exotic; missing is the grit and richness of human reality.

The issue tells us Native Americans had vivid creation myths that gave life meaning; they lived closer to nature than we do on both land and sea (some were politically incorrect and hunted whales and clubbed seals in the Pacific Northwest); and they were somehow in better balance with their surroundings than we are. But nowhere do we get a picture of what such societies truly were: human communities where tragedy and difficult choices, good and evil and the terrors of death, had to be faced and explained. These portraits bear about as much resemblance to their subjects as a *Reader's Digest* story bears to contemporary American life.

In addition to intoning the usual pieties, some of the Native American sentiments expressed in the magazine yearn for historical impossibilities. One woman interviewed in the *National Geographic* spread, for example, laments the loss of her tribe's traditional songs and rituals, as would anyone living with a reduced cultural heritage. But she goes on to register the tragic contradictions of neolithic cultures in tension with modern life: "I am a Christian; I am not sorry the missionaries came. But I wish they had known how to let their news change peoples' lives from the

133

inside, without imposing their culture over our ways."[17] But to be a Christian means precisely that some "ways" are changed, both in attitude and practice, forever. Tragic or not, this is certainly unavoidable.

Religion and Culture

The quandaries of religion and culture are profoundly coupled with serious historical material in the 1991 Canadian film *Black Robe*. *Black Robe* tells the absorbing story of Father Laforgue, an early-seventeenth-century Jesuit missionary to the Hurons who makes a fifteen-hundred-mile canoe trip up Canada's Saint Lawrence River. Exciting and frightening opportunities presented themselves to red and white alike in those early contacts. For the most part, however, these opportunities failed to come to full fruition because of disease, misunderstanding, and profound cultural differences. (We appreciate the difference guns made in native life, but we underestimate, for instance, the importance even steel knives and hatchets had to peoples previously without metals. Natives eagerly traded with the Europeans for them and for woven cloth to replace their animal-skin garments.) The sheer struggle to survive natural and human predators in a harsh environment discouraged all parties from following anything but the most proven ways.

Religion in particular offered a chance for mutual interchange. Though unrecorded in the film, the Jesuits came to have great appreciation for the natural piety of the natives. As we saw in chapter three, the Jesuit *Relations*, the widely read yearly reports priests sent back to their superiors in France, recognize symbolic similarities between Christian sacraments and native rituals, as well as parallels between their stories and those of Scripture. In spite of what they regard as moral shortcomings among the Indians, the black robes saw a possibility for grace to build on nature among woodland tribes. But since whites and Indians alike sought to exploit one another, as we see clearly in *Black Robe*, only

134

something like a religious and cultural confluence would have prevented the sad history that ensued.

Whatever their aesthetic merits, most recent portrayals of European encounters with natives (*Dances With Wolves* being the most popular example) are far less accurate and serious history than *Black Robe*. In fact, they simply reverse the old movie stereotypes of cowboys and Indians. Before, peaceful white settlers bravely confronted a harsh nature and savage tribes to open up an immense land. Now, callous whites disrupt a bountiful nature and nature's aboriginal children, whose lives, by a kind of mirror-image wish-fulfillment, become everything that modern urban life is not—vigorous, free, in harmony with nature. Everything white, including white religion, merely degrades people already living noble lives.

Black Robe, by contrast, takes a stark and independent approach to its subject. It may very well be the best popular representation of the encounter between indigenous peoples and Christianity we will see among quincentenary events. Not only does it include real religion in the story; its generally authentic portrayal of both Europeans and natives has little to do with Eurocentrism or with what we might call aboriginal chic.

To begin with, despite the stunning beauty of its North American woodlands setting, the film never glosses over the hard reality of primitive life. In winter, Indians sleep in cold shelters with open fires that fill the air with smoke. Food is a constant worry, and disease a perpetual specter for which native remedies and medicine men are not sure defenses. This world, as a dying native leader confesses to the priest in the film, is a harsh one; those who live closer to nature than we do know clearly that, for human beings, the physical environment is a sometimes good, sometimes bad relation.

No easy opposition between white and red operates in *Black Robe* either. Some whites are relatively benign; others are not—even to one another. Indians are shown killing and torturing other Indians, as they regularly did throughout tribal societies long before the arrival of the white man. Nor are we given neat divisions between good and bad tribes as in Kevin Costner's *Dances*. Having escaped from a hostile tribe after a bout of torture, an Indian explains to the priest that his tribe is just as brutal. (Perhaps a slight anachronism creeps in here since no native, without the perspective on tribal ways afforded by contact with another culture, would have seen anything much wrong in the perpetual tribal feuds except the inconvenience.)

That such tortures no longer occur in the twentieth century can be attributed, as the film implies, only to the slow and uneven influence of European culture and religion. Tribal society and religion dictated that captives in war had to be treated cruelly as a sign to surrounding tribes of unattackable fierceness. Tribes like the Huron who accepted Christianity after a fashion, and who may have relented to a degree in their use of torture, were simply wiped out by more ruthless tribes like the Iroquois. Suffering genocide was a fearsome price for the Hurons to pay for their turn to better ways. These converts and their martyred missionaries set native cultures, in fits and starts, on a far less bloody course for which we all—white and red alike—should be deeply grateful. Unfortunately, this gradual improvement was later marred by the atrocities of white men themselves.

Native religion receives sympathetic treatment in *Black Robe* but not the blanket acceptance now common in most works of popular culture. The Europeans are half-intrigued, half-repelled by native belief in dreams and wood spirits. Native Americans clearly have belief systems encompassing this world and the next, which are not easily refuted. At the same time the native shaman cuts a rather silly figure as he tries to ward off the evil spirits he thinks the priest brings with him. And we overhear the Iroquois discussing the sacrifice of one of their captives to a war god the next day. (In fact, the Iroquois sometimes went raiding as far as the Dakotas in search of victims for such sacrifices.) While these are small touches, and perhaps not sufficient to correct some widespread misconceptions, they are of crucial importance in accurately presenting native belief and practice.

EVENTS AND COUNTER-EVENTS

Tunnel Vision

Just how unusual and necessary even this small critical treatment is may be appreciated by comparing it with the situation on most college campuses today. Princeton's highly popular course in Native American religions, mentioned in chapter four, is typical of courses around the country. And as at Princeton, professors elsewhere also complain not of student resistance to native ideas but of their uncritical embrace of native religion. We can probably imagine the type of student that usually studies Native American religion today—a student who thinks of native spirituality as a multicultural antidote to civilization. If it got the attention it deserves, *Black Robe* might be a useful antidote to that false multiculturalism.

Unfortunately, even the few people who have seen *Black Robe* do not always comprehend its lessons. Some, as Peter Steinfels has pointed out in the *New York Times*, see it as a chronicle of the Jesuit priest's slow recognition of the validity of Indian culture.[18] This interpretation is simply wrong; we never see any such thing. Yet many young people, apparently assuming that this exceptional creation is just one more item in the monolith of popular culture, interpret *Black Robe* as a kind of homage to Native American wisdom and nobility.

Perhaps more worrisome is the pox-on-both-your-houses approach of urbane critics like the *New York Times*'s Vincent Canby who view the whole story as a pointless disaster for both sides: the Jesuits were ineffective and the Hurons were wiped out.[19] That reading assumes a superiority to and distance from the historical actors that is not warranted. In one astonishing scene Father Laforgue demonstrates to his Algonquian guides how writing works. He takes down a sentence, walks over to a French colleague, and asks him to read it aloud. The Indians draw back in some fear at this inexplicable witchcraft. Yet without the individuals who were willing to carry that witchcraft to unknown peoples at great personal inconvenience, the descendants of those Native Americans would be in no position to read Vincent Canby in the

137

New York Times today. While they might be the better for that particular incapacity, would they be better off isolated from the rest of the world's knowledge and cultures by being unable to read?

Lacking writing, most natives would now not even be well acquainted with their own past. The complaint that whites have written the histories of the Americas has a basis in truth because Europeans were the only people involved who could have *written* the history at all. The Mayas had a writing system, the Aztecs a few pictorial "books," but nowhere in the Americas were there written histories as we understand histories. In fact, as in other parts of the world, European historical interests have retrieved or preserved much of native culture that would have been lost. What survives among still-living native peoples is for the most part too mixed up now with European ways to be taken as always historically authentic.

While scholarly interest may seem small consolation for peoples who have suffered unjustly at the hands of Europeans for five hundred years, past injustice should not be compounded by distorting what remains of native cultures to suit the purposes of various interested parties living now. Anyone—even a Native American—who looks fairly into the history of the tribes that existed when the first Europeans arrived will conclude that resurrecting them as they were would not be a good idea. Neither would resurrecting every aspect of seventeenth-century European culture be very attractive. But many disaffected Westerners are turning to Native Americans as the last available candidates for utopian dreams. The terrible disfigurements of Native American history those utopian impulses will produce should concern Native Americans as much as anyone.

Another American Path

The reaction to *Black Robe*, however, seems to indicate that the myth of the noble savage is likely to mark popular culture for about as long as his counterpart, the ignoble savage, did earlier.

138

Perhaps the most widespread reaction among those who did not simply read the film as part of the zeitgeist was frustration that it did not take sides. What we still fail to appreciate in our common American past is the agonistic nature of all human movements. Should the Europeans who came to the Americas simply have left them as they were? Or, even under the best of circumstances, would the natural evangelical nature of Christianity have made that seem intolerable and a grave lapse of moral responsibility?

Accusations that white Eurocentric thought has distorted the study of Native American cultures usually arise when these issues come up. (Another sin, however, has been the simple neglect of native peoples—a neglect that implies those peoples lack value in the American context.) Even careful anthropologists are seen as guilty of either subtly or crudely imposing meanings by the very tools of their scholarly trade and assigning value to native phenomena. By definition, then, the only impartial and correct views of Native American cultures must come from Native Americans themselves.

On the face of it, this is an odd claim that would be made in few other cases. We may well believe, for example, that the British understand something about their own culture that we Americans, despite a closely related culture and language, do not. Monarchy certainly seems to mean something to them that, after all explanations have been made, still remains a mystery for us. But that does not stop us, or anyone else, from criticizing English stuffiness, bland cuisine, and addiction to interminable cricket matches. The British themselves make kindred criticisms. When we turn to native cultures, however, a sort of *noblesse oblige* seems to intervene. Not only do we fail to treat Native Americans as moral and intellectual equals, a condescending attitude arises that distorts the very examination of native culture. In any culture—be it the culture of the United States or the former Soviet Union, of South Africa or South Yemen—we know that positive and negative qualities will be mixed in differing proportions. Good and evil traits are indigenous to every human society.

Yet Native American cultures seem to be excluded from this

universal rule. When many contemporary scholars, politicians, activists, clergy, journalists, and just plain folks turn to these cultures, an odd thing happens. Suddenly, the tradition of intellectual and journalistic professions to question everything vanishes, and we are overwhelmed with pleas to "respect" certain cultures without debate. While for some people the disparity between the average incomes of men and of women in the United States is an abomination, and calling attention to the deep structures that perpetuate it is a duty, pointing out the low position of women, incessant tribal warfare, torture of captives, and enslavement that existed in most pre-colonial North American Indian cultures is disrespectful. Such facts have been horribly used, moreover, to justify the white man's mistreatment and genocide of the red man.

Merely to raise these issues is to run the risk of placing oneself outside the bounds of civil discourse. After all, whatever the Native Americans did to one another, doesn't it pale in comparison to what whites did to them? Furthermore, because Native Americans now are in sad shape, wouldn't additional criticism simply be cruel? Doesn't moral seriousness require us to be more concerned about respect for Indian traditions than to bring up old issues that may well feed stereotypes?

Answering yes to the three questions just posed is taken as a sign of sophistication and transcendence of Eurocentric categories. But is it? Is it not, rather, a failure akin to the failure to appreciate ancient Israel's warring kings, or Japan's shoguns, or India's moguls? Instead of paying respect to alien traditions—the respect of presenting them and trying to understand them in their fullness—doesn't this patronizing attitude reduce them all to bland caricatures, props for contemporary quarrels?

It need not be so. Seriously studying native cultures with sympathy need not lead to one-sided readings of history. In fact, at Berkeley, where a "diversity" requirement has introduced students to previously unfamiliar material about the history of native America, students seem to be coming to appreciate historical complexities and paradoxes. In one class, Berkeley students discussed Joel S. Martin's *Sacred Revolt*, a study of Muskogee

Indians and their resistance to white influences around 1800.[20] Like many other Indian groups the Muskogee had slaves and certain patriarchal social structures. A woman in the class complained that the text underemphasized how "women were being oppressed while a black student objected to the facile disposal of the question of slavery by saying that slaves were treated better in Indian villages than on white plantations."[21] Such reactions indicate that attempts to face past injustices need not lead to the creation of new intellectual injustices.

But the concern should spread beyond trendy feminist and racial preoccupations. The Muskogean Natchez of the U.S. southeastern woodlands lived in a rigid society of four castes, practiced human sacrifice, and killed the wives of upper-caste ("Great Sun") males out of grief when they died, a kind of Natchez suttee.[22] Knowing these facts and their connection to Indian culture and belief systems should lead us to look outside or beyond what is of contemporary salience to even broader questions, to "the other" in all his glory and horror. What good effects have new modes of thought brought to many of the Native Americans themselves? This kind of multiculturalism, however, would have no time for sentimental pieties about respect for indigenous ways that do not warrant respect.

Elementary-School Distortions

If Berkeley students could see only part of the problem, what about students not as mature? They are often subjected to one-sided presentations they can hardly be expected to notice, much less resist. In the fall of 1991, for example, an issue of *Scholastic Update*, a typical grade-school-level newsletter on current events, decided to stimulate discussion about the Columbus anniversary under the familiar rubric "Separating the Man from the Myth."[23] In a sense, *Scholastic* does present different views, but it also leaves the overwhelming impression—and at this age impressions, not critical thought, are more formative of future opinions—that

141

Columbus was a brute who does not even have the honor of being the first European to arrive here.

Typical of many similar efforts to separate myth from reality, the discussion includes very little about Columbus and his actions at all. He appears only in a sketchy three-page overview that crudely sets out some of the historical material. The rest of the issue is devoted to how different countries like Spain, Mexico, and the Dominican Republic feel about 1992, how young Native Americans feel about themselves (they want and do not want to be part of white culture), and how all of us should feel about the environmental crisis. The magazine asserts (falsely) that the Spaniards entirely wiped out the Aztecs and Incas. It also lingers over one reporter's visits to the Yanomani, a still-intact tribe in the Brazilian Amazon that has become an international cause célèbre almost on a par with the undisturbed rainforest itself. The Yanomani have been so isolated that they remain susceptible to "European" diseases and disruptions. They are described as displaying a profound knowledge of their environment in one paragraph, but this appears in another:

> The Yanomani believe that their god, Omame, deserted them when the white men invaded their soil. Kopenawa, another Yanomani leader, offered an explanation for the onslaught of malaria in the region.
>
> "Omame put the minerals below the earth because it is cold," he said. "Then came the miners and [they] took out the minerals. When the minerals came out into the hot air, it [sic] turned to poison and spread many diseases. The miners don't know they are spreading poison to the world. The world will end, will die."

After reading this mythological account, intelligent American schoolchildren may be puzzled about the pious assertions on another page that Indians are serious caretakers of the earth who "can't do it alone anymore."

The single page in *Scholastic Update* devoted to "debate" does not even attempt to engage issues. It merely allows space for certified and predictable voices to be heard: Houston Baker (black), Mario Cuomo (Italian), Antonia Hernandez (Mexican American/woman), Wilma Mankiller (chief, Cherokee Nation), and Patrick Buchanan (presumably, pugnacious Eurocentrist). Students learn elsewhere in the newsletter that Indian groups will be sending ships from New York City to Spain to claim it as Native American territory, that protests are planned against the replicas of Columbus's ships sailing to San Salvador for October 1992 and stopping before and after in other cities, and that 1992 has been declared the Year of Indigenous Peoples—by indigenous peoples. Absent other information, even an adult would have a hard time knowing what to think about Columbus after reading all this. A twelve- or thirteen-year-old will be left with little historical information with which to separate the man from either the myth or the anti-myth.

National Leadership in Education

It is hardly surprising that *Scholastic Update* should have spurned Columbus himself and approached 1492 from the angle of current ethnic tensions, however, since that is precisely what many of the most prestigious educational and professional organizations in the country have advocated. The National Council on the Social Studies (along with almost thirty signatories drawn from educational, scholarly, and professional organizations) prepared a brief position statement in 1991 for use by educators: *The Columbian Quincentenary: An Educational Opportunity* contains some very good suggestions set in a less-than-ideal framework.[24] The council makes two major recommendations. The second suggestion— that students should be provided with "basic accurate knowledge about Columbus's voyages, their historical setting, and unfolding effects"—has an unobjectionable, even laudable aim. Unfortunately, it follows on the heels of the more dubious recommendation that teachers "help students comprehend the contemporary relevance of 1492"—in short, not to read history but to read current issues into history.

Were it not for the fact that the contemporary relevance has already been determined, even the latter aim might be a relatively benign or enlightening undertaking. But we know that historical objectivity now often succumbs to other interests when Europe figures centrally in a story, as it does in this one. In fact, the statement admits that "the world as we know it would not have come to be were it not for the chain of events set in motion by European contact with the Americas." Yet out of fear that "public hyperbole," meaning uncritical adulation of Columbus, will dominate the anniversary, the council issues several cautions.

First, Columbus must be understood in the context of a contemporary multi-ethnic and culturally pluralistic United States with ties to all other parts of the world. While this America should be regarded as "one of history's first universal or world nations," however, it should not be seen as having anything that places it above other nations or cultures. Here, the council crosses into the ghostly world of global education. As currently practiced, global education does not so much teach facts in order that students in the various parts of the world may understand one another. Rather, the goal of global education is to lead students to some sort of disembodied, neutral point of view vis-à-vis all the nations and cultures of the world. In this vision the United States becomes nothing more than a respectful receptacle of various other cultures that of course, in their turn, have great intrinsic value.

Second, the council advises teachers to provide students with a fuller account of the history of the Americas prior to 1492. That history should not be regarded as a virtual blank, but a story of

> highly developed agricultural systems, centers of dense populations, complex civilizations, large-scale empires, extensive networks of long-distance trade and cultural diffusion, complex patterns of interstate conflict and cooperation, sophisticated systems of religious and scientific belief, extensive linguistic diversity, and regional variations in the levels of societal complexity.

All this, as we have argued in previous chapters, is quite true and a much-needed corrective to past neglect. Yet, set as it is in the council's framework, the directive gives the impression that white Europeans simply ignored a wealth of historical information available in native form. But were it not for the white Europeans who have re-created much of it, this history would have remained all but unknown to native populations and others alike. The fact that political appreciation of such knowledge lagged behind scholarship should not blind us to the basic openness of European culture and its interest in the cultures of the others.

So strong is the council's desire for all parties to have an equal role in this story, however, that the obvious lead of Europe, conceded at the document's beginning, is denied in the subsequent enumeration of groups that have made up the Americas. Native Americans and Africans, we are told, were not merely passive victims of Europeans—a true statement within limits. But then the limits are entirely ignored:

> All parties pursued their interests as they perceived them—
> sometimes independently of the interests of others, sometimes
> in collaboration with others, and sometimes in conflict with
> others. All borrowed from and influenced the others and, in
> turn, were influenced by them. The internal diversity of the
> Native Americans, the Africans, and the Europeans contributed
> to the development of modern American pluralistic culture and
> contemporary world civilization.

If this was true, one begins to wonder, why are Native American and African-American groups complaining? Of course, in a very general way, everyone "contributed" to what is now America. But the desire to credit everyone equally here blurs the fact, evident to any dispassionate historian, that for both good and bad Europe is central, no less for its sins than as the unique source of the concepts of pluralism, human rights, and democracy that we value in the Americas.

The peoples of the Americas caused the Europeans to do some rethinking (see chapter three), and the National Council on the Social Studies might have done well to include that history in its observations and recommended bibliography. Its failure to do so

145

exacts a heavy toll. Interpreting the "contemporary relevance of 1492" in current political, ethnic, and racial terms only obscures the origins of the very ideas that seek to guarantee liberty and justice to all. Those origins are lost and falsely seen as having emerged almost impersonally from the bare contact of different peoples. The council is no worse in this regard than many other groups examining the quincentenary, but its responsibility is greater. It encourages teachers to leave students exactly where they started—vaguely oriented toward a vague universalism but lacking any idea of the sources of the precious legacy of freedom, however flawed and incomplete, they have inherited.

A common utopian aim seems to hover over many organizations and individuals concerned with 1492—from those solemnly planning the nature funeral on San Salvador to those shaping educational curricula. That aim may be clearly discerned in the telling and emblematic debut in early 1992 of the film *Medicine Man*.[25] Its protagonist, played by Sean Connery, is a medical researcher in the Brazilian rainforest who discovers there, not only the healing properties of native life, but a cure for cancer. Physical, emotional, social, and environmental factors meld together as he seeks to fend off the ridiculously exaggerated brutal advances of exploitative road-builders. Fire caused by the evil whites destroys Connery's village and drug supply, but he will follow his tribe and continue his quest, reversing the direction of five hundred years of European and American history. The symbolic point of this not-very-well-made moral tale cannot be missed. In fact, Connery's young female assistant announces it openly: the hero hasn't found just a cure for cancer, he's discovered "the cure for the disease of the twentieth century."

146

6

Democratic Vistas

Heaven have mercy on us all—Presbyterians and
Pagans alike—for we are somehow dreadfully cracked
about the head.

—Herman Melville
Moby Dick

In early 1992 the city council of Berkeley, California, declared
unanimously that October 12 would no longer be celebrated as
Columbus Day but as Indigenous Peoples' Day. One leader of
Resistance 500, the task force heading the coalition that sought the
change, explained the vote in terms that would be attractive to
many Americans in the approach to the quincentenary: "It's
moving from a philosophy of war, imperialism, and exploitation
of peoples and lands personified by people like Columbus and the
conquerors to a philosophy of living in peace and harmony with
neighbors and different cultures."[1] Though the Berkeley declaration begs several difficult questions and surely reflects no serious
attempt to become acquainted with the history of Columbus or
Native Americans, it was a trendy—almost predictable—political
move. By making it, the Berkeley City Council confronts us with
the kind of received wisdom that should be examined carefully if
we wish to understand the civic dimension of the controversies
over 1492 and the past five hundred years.

If the council had decided simply to highlight the need for
mainstream America to accord greater recognition to Native

147

American citizens, and for finding a better *modus vivendi* among our diverse peoples, it would not have generated much interest or disagreement. In recent decades Native Americans—like many other U.S. minority communities—have found a new acceptance within traditional majorities. The minorities proudly celebrate their many contributions to the common culture and see those achievements reflected in textbooks, politics, and the media. In the 1990 census a much larger number of people identified themselves as Native Americans than ever before. Why this is so remains unclear, but ethnic pride and, paradoxically, social advantage in an increasingly open United States seem to be two important factors. Though minority leaders have at times abused this openness and provoked some backlash by taking extreme, aggressive positions that most of their own people do not support, by and large the status of minorities is probably at an all-time high in U.S. history. The desire to mark that status on the calendar and remind us all of the social failures yet to be remedied, then, does not come as much of a surprise.

Perhaps the most emblematic and disturbing aspect of the Berkeley decision is that it *replaced* the Columbus holiday with the indigenous peoples' celebration—a step that represents not an addition but an intentional affront to traditional European culture. Furthermore, as the Resistance 500 member's explanation made evident, this step stems from the belief that native peoples surpassed Europeans in their capacity to live in harmony with one another and with nature. Rightly or wrongly, a sizable group of Americans today feels that we have lost our social links with one another and are seriously damaging the natural environment. These dissatisfactions color perceptions of both Native American and European ways. And they underlie the public receptiveness to what is believed to be native wisdom. Popular assumptions about the inherent virtues of indigenous tribes, however, as we have seen in previous chapters, rest on shaky—sometimes nonexistent— historical ground and often distort the very cultures that many people profess to value.

148

DEMOCRATIC VISTAS

Use and Abuse of "History"

Unfortunately, several widespread notions about traditional Native American life are literal fictions. Just one indication of how they may be artificially contrived surfaced in early 1992 when the nineteenth-century Indian sage Chief Seattle was invoked on Earth Day. For some time the chief has been identified as a visionary and an eloquent speaker who commented on the issues many middle-class Americans now find most worrisome—the environment and social tensions. Accordingly, the organizers of Earth Day 1992 (April 22) encouraged religious and political leaders to read a letter Chief Seattle had supposedly written in 1854 to U.S. President Franklin Pierce. Among other concerns in the letter, the chief proclaims the earth to be our mother and complains, "I have seen a thousand rotting buffaloes on the prairies left by the white man who shot them from a passing train." The entire letter confirms widespread current beliefs about the relations of Indian and white man, about Indian wisdom and white rapacity.

The principal problem with these beliefs, however, is that they often have no basis in fact. In this case Chief Seattle never wrote those words. His home was six hundred miles from the nearest buffalo, and the letter is dated fifteen years before the railroad arrived in the Northwest. But even though Earth Day U.S.A. officials had heard reports that the letter might be inauthentic, they decided to send it out to religious leaders anyway as "attributed" to Chief Seattle.

And indeed it had been, in an odd way, by a modern white religious institution. The words in the fictional letter were actually created by Ted Perry, a Texas scriptwriter, for a 1971 film produced by the Southern Baptist Radio and Television Commission. The commission wanted to give a warning about the environment and thought it would be appropriate to have Chief Seattle make the plea. Unfortunately, many viewers assumed that the film's moving environmental sentiments had been pronounced by Seattle himself, and several institutions publicized them through various channels as his—a mistake that angered both Perry and

149

historians of northwestern indigenous peoples. Though this comedy of errors may be unusual in degree, such contemporary use (or misuse) of a revered Indian figure as a ventriloquist's dummy is by no means unique. General public ignorance about specific Native American groups makes it easy to attribute to them just about any notion that seems progressive without much fear of contradiction. How popular sentiments toward Native Americans will be affected when the truth eventually becomes known is another story. Just as Columbus found himself embroiled with people to whom he had oversold the ease with which wealth could be gotten in the New World, those who oversell the Native American heritage may be inviting deep disillusionment.

As these revelations about the letter were coming out, *Brother Eagle, Sister Sky*, a children's book on the environment based on Chief Seattle's spurious sayings, was number five on the *New York Times* bestseller list. Questioned about that volume's authenticity, its illustrator told the *New York Times*, "Basically, I don't know what he said—but I do know that the Native American people lived this philosophy, and that's what's important."[2] Which native peoples lived what philosophy, or even the barest outlines of the chief's real views, do not seem to interest people who have already decided—independently of any evidence or historical study— what Native American cultures were in the past and what they mean in the present.

Chief Seattle was, in fact, a baptized Roman Catholic who had eight Indian slaves—in time-honored Northwest Indian tradition —until Lincoln's Emancipation Proclamation. Though he earned a reputation as a bold raider against surrounding tribes, he probably had some deep and sensible things to say about relations between red and white men. But the president of the company who published *Brother Eagle, Sister Sky* appeared to have no interest in any of this, dismissing charges of inaccuracy by saying, "For want of a tape recorder [presumably to have properly recorded Chief Seattle's original words] maybe we have a book that will change children's view about the environment." Giving those same children false and misleading information about a Native

American leader and his culture did not seem to trouble her as long as it served a cause white society regarded as good.

Multitudinously Native

As part of the rich variety of native cultures in the Americas, over three hundred different Indian tribes existed within what is now the United States alone. Even using the word "tribes" to describe these diverse groups cannot begin to convey the range of peoples and social forms between North America's two coasts. Near present-day St. Louis, for example, mound-builders raised enormous structures, probably temples, in the midst of a large, fixed urban complex. Contemporaneous with the Cahokian mound-builders, whaling peoples on the Northwest Coast, nomadic tribes in the interior, and numerous other nations dwelled in these lands. The complexity of this country's Native American history far exceeds any one person's capacity to know.

Several immovable obstacles, moreover, stand in the way—the lack of written native languages being primary among them. We must rely almost entirely on oral traditions and archeological evidence, where available, to reconstruct Native American history. Often these two sources do not confirm each other. Later accretions to oral histories and gaps in the physical evidence introduce uncertainties everywhere. The written testimony of European settlers helps but inevitably contains inaccuracies and downright misunderstandings, though it is receiving renewed attention.[3] Given the vigorous economic, political, and military interaction of native peoples, all these instruments, even combined, still leave much to be desired. It is as if we had to reconstruct several centuries of Italian Renaissance history, not from the documents of the warring city-states, but from the anecdotal accounts of Arab traders who had contacts with Genoa, Venice, Florence, or Naples.

In addition to this fragmented situation, the more politicized assertions regarding the abilities of Indians to live harmoniously with one another and with nature, which may be supported by evidence from one tribe, can be quite easily contradicted by evidence of different practices in other tribes. The Natchez Indians, as we have seen, had social hierarchies and slavery; the Sanpoils, who lived on the Columbia River, practiced absolute equality and pacifism. Pacifism, of course, was a rarity among indigenous peoples. The Sanpoils were highly unusual and fortunate in that they were able to preserve their equality and pacifism between two very different types of societies: those on the Northwest Coast with rigid social structures and those on the Great Plains marked by bellicosity.[4] Yet, in a sense, Carlos Fuentes is right to claim that all these peoples act as a "buried mirror" in which we may see our own mixed and partly obscured features more readily.

Iroquois Democracy and Imperialism

Contradictory traits sometimes show up within the same indigenous group. The Iroquois had probably the most highly developed Native American political association in North America, and much has been written of their achievements. DeWitt Clinton called them the "Romans of the West" because of their "martial spirit" and their "rage for conquest." The so-called Iroquois Confederation—the nascent civic structure of the Seneca, Onondaga, Oneida, Mohawk, and Cayuga—arrived at peaceful and relatively democratic relations within the Five Nations. In 1987 the U.S. Congress formally proclaimed that the Iroquois played an important role in the creation of American democracy. As a result, American schoolchildren are taught today that the Iroquois Confederation was a model for the American Founders when they began to consider how to organize the thirteen independent former colonies.

Controversy is widespread among historians over whether this is a historical fact. A few—very few—passages show that the Founders were, of course, aware of the confederation. Ben Franklin probably captures the spirit of how most of the Founders felt about the question in his remarks on the need for a Union:

> It would be a very strange Thing, if . . . Nations of ignorant Savages should be capable of forming a Scheme for such a Union, and be able to execute it in such a Manner, as that it has subsisted Ages, and appears indissoluble; and yet a like Union should be impracticable for ten or a Dozen Colonies.[5]

Franklin's combination of disparagement ("ignorant Savages") and admiration (suggesting "a *like* Union") reflects the vague interest typical of his times. Not until the 1840s did anyone investigate the actual structure of the confederation. Consequently, its role in shaping the Constitution in any serious way is doubtful to say the least.[6]

In any case, outside the constituent Iroquoian groups, the confederation practiced what can only be called an imperial policy towards other peoples. Francis Jennings, an appreciative student of Indian cultures, has written that the Iroquois, because of their political structure, considered themselves the wisest of Indians and "rationalized their role of hegemony over other tribes. It was for the latter's own good—not an unfamiliar argument among imperialists."[7] The British called the heavily fortified Iroquois villages "castles"—a further indication of the kinds of relations that existed among tribes long before the white man added his evils.

E pluribus plures

Ethnocentrism in the Americas was not unique to Europeans and Iroquois, either. We are appalled at the abuse, physical and verbal, that Europeans visited upon Native Americans, and no amount of historical explanation can ever excuse behavior that the Europeans themselves should have recognized was an outrage. Yet Native Americans visited a great deal of abuse on one another as well, as their languages reveal. Most Indian groups regarded only themselves as full human beings and members of other tribes as inferior in customs or understanding. The Algonquians called the Iroquois army the "Nation of Snakes." Jennings points out that we do not always possess even a good idea of the actual names of certain groups, and not only because of the lack of written records:

"Clarity is not helped by the ethnocentricity of the tribes. They did not hesitate to refer to their hostile neighbors with pejoratives equivalent to 'stinker' and 'cannibals.'"[8] The Taínos, whom Columbus encountered in his first contacts and thought were living in natural harmony, had a lower class from "the place of people without merit," as they called it.[9]

At one time settlers justified their own actions toward natives by citing native atrocities toward one another. Both the Dutch and the British, for instance, bought land from Indians who had recently driven off other Indians—a native usurpation that set a bad example for some Europeans only too ready to believe that "primitive" peoples had no rights.[10] The record of intertribal warfare should never have been used in that way. It is the moral equivalent of saying that because some Frenchmen steal from one another, it is all right for Englishmen to steal from Frenchmen. The whole exercise is a moral muddle that shows bad faith on the part of the excuse-maker. What the historical record does indicate, however, is that Berkeley's proponents of "living in harmony with neighbors and different cultures" have not really looked into Native American cultures. Even Columbus's gentle Taínos had earlier "displaced" the Guanahacabibes and drew him into the long-standing warfare among Caribbean tribes.[11] But modern Columbus critics continue to invoke on faith peaceful "indigenous peoples," as if these were a consistent and common entity rather than a collection of distinctive groups with divergent mores and interests, often in sharp conflict with one another.

In fact, it is only fair to point out to modern admirers of tribal systems that they carry within them some of the very problems that contemporary critics of America find most annoying. Tribal systems, almost by definition, exist by sharply delineating those within from those outside the kinship system, though kinship among most Native Americans is a primarily social, rather than biological, concept. Tribes often adopted captured members of other tribes, including whites, to replace their own members who had died or been killed in battle. After a particularly severe decline in population, for example, the Iroquois adopted the entire Tuscarora tribe. A tribe usually consisted of all those who were born or had formally been inducted into it. Yet the entire cultural formation of those within, of whatever biological background, distinguished them from those without. The Iroquois tribes stopped perpetrating cannibalism on one another after forming their confederation, but continued it, along with torture, against captives from other tribes. Those who find modern mainstream America horribly exclusive and its treatment of various groups outrageously inequitable might benefit from some exposure to comparative ethnology.[12]

Furthermore, while open to integrating others in certain circumstances, tribal practices at their core represent the very opposite of cultural openness. Outsiders were accepted in many groups, but only in so far as they accepted and participated in the monolithic culture of the tribe. The cultural pluralism that we value so highly did not exist within any tribe. And the various tribes in North America, taken together, made up a diverse group only in that each preserved itself as a separate entity, mostly in opposition to others, within a certain land area. In this there is not much of a lesson for a contemporary America seeking the meaning of *e pluribus unum*. Rather, it would seem to caution us that the current equivalent of tribal animosities, which are fostered by separate social elements who do not wish to be part of any larger whole and who are willing to defend their separatism militantly, threaten the generally peaceful fabric of American civic life.

The Many Forms of Myth

Another way of looking at current attempts to find a lost paradise in native America, however, is to recall the enduring myth we cited in the introduction. Since the beginning of the European arrival, Americans have been tempted to think, as David Noble has shown, that they can escape from the "the terror of historical change to live in timeless harmony with nature." That myth used to conjure up biblical images of the Garden of Eden, but after two hundred years of national existence, many Americans see both Judaism and Christianity as too deeply intertwined with the past to help much with historical terrors. Instead, they turn to Native Americans and their cultures for a pre-historical— i.e., non-historical, and therefore unsullied—set of beliefs and behaviors that can fill the gap in the old white European psyche.

But that need can be met, of course, only if Native Americans are not scrutinized too closely. Native America, as its defenders sometimes claim, has a history as well. And like all human history Indian history cannot be studied in any depth without disenchantment: there was no utopian garden; there were numerous epic and tragic events. Even a superficial reading of indigenous epics, prophecies, and songs reveals as much. Furthermore, Native American myth provides little guidance for alleviating contemporary American woes. Understanding the various stories and rituals of widely differing Indian tribes may lead us to appreciate the human wisdom and often witty invention encapsulated in their oral traditions. But in the modern world there is an unbridgeable chasm between them and us. Just as we may appreciate certain truths formulated in ancient Greek myths about Athena, Aphrodite, Zeus, and Hera, so we may learn from stories about Raven, Coyote, Fox, and Changing Woman—but only with the most willing suspension of disbelief. For most of us these tales can be only broadly edifying and in no way offer otherwise unattainable solutions to contemporary crises.

The very term myth already relegates the phenomenon it describes to a status somewhere between truth and fiction. There are "true" fictions after a fashion, but when we deal with ultimate questions, we want to know more than whether a given system provides moral or spiritual light; we want to know whether it fully represents reality. Because the stories of creation in Genesis and in a few Native American myths cannot be falsified by any scientific discovery, they are universal and enduring. But other creation stories—such as those in which the earth rises from the movements of a turtle stirring up sand from the bottom of primordial waters or (with the Aztecs) solidifies from the blood of the gods—exist in another realm. The Western impulse to give

156

equal value to all cultures has limits; these stories are not in the same category as Genesis, any more than are the stories in the early Western tradition. In Homer black-winged Night joins with the Wind and lays a silver egg from which emerges Eros, double-sexed, golden-winged, having four heads, and the source of motion in the universe.[13] This is a Western story in which we may no longer "believe" except in the most esoteric sense and only after considerable modern exegesis.

Frank recognition of myth as myth is important in the Columbus controversies. General claims about the value of Native American spirituality rarely acknowledge the filtering process that separates from its full original context what we consider to be useful for us now. Belief and practice were highly integrated in native societies, and preserving one part of the system absent others is no easy matter. In violence-prone modern urban America, few people who praise native cultures would be willing to reinstate North American male puberty rites intimately tied to hunting and warfare. Nor would many people concerned with the status of women be likely to embrace the corresponding female rituals:

> Puberty rites for girls usually correlated with their biological maturity—the onset of menstruation. Isolated from their communities, these girls had to observe many personal restrictions, such as not touching their own flesh lest they mar their beauty; drinking only through a straw to prevent causing an excess of rain; avoiding the food and belongings of men, especially hunters, lest they weaken them; and practicing benevolence, humility, and proper demeanor.[14]

Though it would be unfair to suggest that these elements exhaust any native group's conceptions of male and female roles, the problem we face is clear. Whenever we recommend native practices, we pick and choose from among them those that are in harmony with the needs of the present. We do the selecting, moreover, on the basis of a value system that most of us would consider universal, not simply the product of Eurocentric thought.

Double Standards

It is curious that the critiques of militarism and power, fixed gender roles and social taboos, which are vigorously applied to delegitimize Western cultures, are almost never directed toward native societies that were clearly as enmeshed in these universal human issues as we are. An odd tendency runs through much scholarly writing on Native Americans. On the one hand, we are led through complex facts about their societies to show us that they, too, had developed social forms often, it is implied, superior to our own. On the other hand, many facets of these societies are tacitly accepted, or explained, in ways that would never be permitted in the discussion of any Western system.

One typical anthropologist, for example, praises the communitarianism of native societies in which persons "took their identity from membership in various groups and had little or no independent status apart from society. Hence, the self was not a unique entity, but rather the intersection of family lines, social positions, and spiritual bonds, all intended to serve the whole community."[15] While this degree of connectedness to a community may sound comforting to modern Americans who find society too fragmented and individualistic, is a self that is solely the product of and subordinate to society something we wish to embrace without further discussion? The social fit is so perfect that we may even grow suspicious: perhaps what is being described is not so much what was, but what we in large, industrialized, urban societies would wish a vigorous life in face-to-face communities close to nature might be. The writer quoted above seems to confirm such suspicions when, after spending most of a long essay emphasizing the ties to a responsible and benevolent community, he suddenly—without explanation and in contradiction to massive historical evidence—announces that "all the [North American] societies tolerated a wide range of personal freedom and gender variations."[16] What happened to indigenous caste systems, socialization, and slavery? And what about the self that was "not a unique entity"?

The impression from much literature on Indians is that they are a blank sheet of paper on which to write various contemporary *desiderata*. Thinkers who would denounce priestcraft and oppression in medieval Catholicism, for example, seem to have no trouble defending native shamans, who directed entire communities, on the grounds that they acted out of traditional knowledge and benevolence. But some of their actual behavior may give us pause. Much like an ancient Christian catechumen, a Keresan boy growing up in a pueblo was gradually introduced to the mysteries of his religion. But there the similarity ends. Anthropologists report blithely that the penalty for revealing to women or children that men dress up as the kachinas, or tribal gods, was beheading.[17]

While all these historical studies involve countless complexities, even this brief examination clearly makes us realize that Indian cultures do not provide a simple reservoir of social or religious value upon which we may draw without careful discernment. And this realization should help us better understand the early North American settlers' errors and misreadings of native culture and intentions.

Corporate Relations

We are constantly being told that those cultures contain vast deposits of wisdom if we could only discover them. In fact, it might be truer to say that we should approach all such promises of lost riches with caution. We know now, for example, that most Algonquians and Iroquois along the Atlantic coast with whom the first settlers came into contact viewed intergroup relations as basically corporate. We tend to project onto these social arrangements idealistic portraits of solidarity within and unity outside the group. While some individuals—red and white—occasionally established personal relationships with members of the opposite group, group mentalities, misunderstandings, and reciprocal atrocities greatly hampered good developments. Indiscriminate white retaliation for red acts is now familiar to even grade-school children; the converse is not.

Algonquian and Iroquoian tribal culture had long sanctioned corporate revenge. If a neighboring tribe killed warriors, their wives were entitled to demand capture of other men to fill their places. Seizing men from another tribe, of course, usually required killing several more, which began another round of warfare because the second tribe would then call for captives to replace their own lost warriors. Under the circumstances it is no wonder that warfare could seem perpetual.

Indian-white relations often fell into a similar pattern. In the early North American contacts during the sixteenth century, Indians would hold responsible any white for the transgressions of any other. A climate of suspicion and awareness of slights also grew. Natives unfamiliar with markets thought French and other European arguments about price fluctuations were nothing more than excuses for cheating. They tended to regard their own tribe's ways as the best, and their attitudes toward Europeans, despite admiration for European technical accomplishments, were frequently condescending. Indians familiar with the land felt vastly superior to the palefaces who were unable to feed themselves or hunt very well. All told, it is astonishing that Indian-white relations were as good as they were—in more instances than we are inclined to remember today—in the early contacts.[18] Proponents of pre-contact native cultures would do well to consider how corporate approaches to mutual interaction made conflict with Europeans virtually unavoidable, and how facile invocation of group grievances in contemporary society may be returning us to far-from-ideal indigenous conditions. The rioting, looting, and racial revenge that occurred in Los Angeles in 1992 after a controversial jury decision in the Rodney King case showed how easy it is to slip back into indiscriminate corporate retaliation.

Harsh Introductions

"Early contacts" is a concept worth examining in itself. Most Americans, if asked, would probably date the beginnings of the United States from either the English settlement at Jamestown

(1608) or the Pilgrims' at Plymouth (1620). Yet both dates neglect a long history of contacts between Europeans and natives that had already shaped relations here decades before the founding of permanent colonies. When Captain John Smith arrived, he found that the Indians of the Chesapeake Bay had—and were accustomed to—French goods shipped down from Canada. (Jacques Cartier's explorations had taken place in the 1530s, and French influence had grown ever since.) Hoping for advantageous trade relations, Chief Powhatan in Virginia even invited Smith to abandon Jamestown and move the settlement to territory Powhatan controlled.[19] Early contacts in North America, then, consisted of gradually expanding interaction between Indians and Europeans —often stimulated by native desire for goods, trade, and military advantage over traditional enemies—not a sudden and crushing eruption of the latter among the former.

Witness Chief Massasoit's welcoming of the Pilgrims at Plymouth. The Indian Squanto, who introduced the English and acted as an interpreter, was a Patuxent who had been kidnapped by an English sea captain and sold into slavery in Spain (in violation of Spanish law) in 1614. He escaped from Spain to England with the help of another English captain, and later returned to his native land in 1619 to find that his people had been wiped out by an epidemic. Despite all this he promoted and succeeded in establishing good relations between Pilgrims and Indians for some time. One recent analyst of these relations has written:

> For nearly fifty years, the simple treaty of 1620 signed by Massasoit, a sachem representing, it was believed, the entire Wamponoag Federation, and Plymouth's governor John Carver worked splendidly. By the treaty, both parties pledged that they would not "doe hurte" unto the other, a pledge that was maintained throughout extremely provocative and risky times. Then in the 1660s came the cultural disturbances that led to King Phillip's War—the war that totally ruined the peaceful accommodations of two generations of native and English diplomats.[20]

In the current controversies about much larger issues, these fragile first accommodations that might have developed into a more pacific mixed culture are often overlooked, just as Columbus's relations with Guacanagarí are overlooked. Two generations of peaceful relations was no small achievement. While good will or cultural understanding may not have been sufficient on either side to have made the long-term history turn out differently than it did, a rich and fluid situation clearly existed at the time of the first permanent settlements, and opportunities were sometimes taken. Unlike the Spanish, the English never devoted themselves to sustained theological and ethical reflection on the status of natives, but even a thoughtful pursuit of mutual advantage might have led to a far different outcome.

Wilcomb Washburn, a longtime resident scholar at the Smithsonian Institution, denounces the many revolting reactions of Puritans and Virginians to the natives but remarks:

> None of the Indian wars of New England was inevitable—even in the psychological sense . . . and certainly not in an economic sense. . . . Peaceful coexistence between Indian and White was, therefore, possible. Although it did not occur, it was not because of underlying imperatives but because both sides— particularly the English—blundered into confrontations that exploded into full-scale war. . . . In Virginia also peaceful coexistence was possible but did not occur. . . . All the wars of Virginia could have been avoided and the conspiracies made unnecessary if English conduct toward the Indians had equalled the standards of honorable dealing that the Virginia Company and the royal government sought to uphold.[21]

This assessment is more than mere late wishful thinking. Several alliances and treaties, and the slow evolution and increase in mutual trade and understanding, could indeed have yielded a better result. The view that European arrogance and blindness, or the gap between the neolithic natives and the English, made war and destruction inevitable rests on no firm historical basis.

162

What Indian Opinion?

One of the little-told stories about contemporary controversies over the Native American past is the division of opinion within surviving indigenous groups themselves—something we would take for granted in any other U.S. ethnic group. James A. Clifton, an anthropologist who has been involved in recent legal and political battles over tribal rights and entitlement, has recorded some of the complex cleavages that exist among Indians today.[22] Quite often these Indian cleavages mirror cleavages within the rest of American society. While retaining a strong tribal identity, some groups such as the Klamath in Oregon, says Clifton, are prosperous and underwent a relatively smooth process of integration into the mainstream culture. Other groups, such as the Southern Ute of Colorado, have maintained a separate identity on a self-administered reservation but have flourished, largely owing to skillful management. Public discussions of Native American affairs rarely include these success stories.

More familiar to the popular consciousness is another type of group Clifton has studied. The Prairie Potowatomi Indians, for example, are very poor and deeply divided internally, making it virtually impossible for them to formulate or pursue a coherent tribal policy. In their efforts to get political and economic relief, they become involved in endless legal struggles that disregard their particular history and anthropology. Clifton summarizes their aims: "obtaining absolute political autarchy while perpetuating absolute fiscal dependence."[23]

The tribal situation perhaps least understood in the public mind, however, is illustrated by the Menominee in Wisconsin. The tribe voted years ago to accept a terminal financial settlement and to disband itself as a formal entity under government support. But as the mood among Indian leaders throughout the nation altered and pressure built for all indigenous groups to reassert their identities, the Menominee were moved to consider "retribalization." Clifton, who was then administering a VISTA-like program in Wisconsin, was confronted with three large Menominee factions:

163

1. Restorationists—"mainly educated middle-class, off-reservation women . . . the protégées of the liberal wing of Wisconsin's Democratic Party, spurred on also by flotsam on the rising tide of militant paleface feminism";

2. Terminationists—"all elder, mainly male, upper middle-class managers and entrepreneurs . . . aided and abetted by the conservative wing of Wisconsin's Republican Party";

3. Warriors Society—"mainly young, urban, lower-class males and the women who adored them . . . covertly coached in their deftly played confrontational tactics by a political splinter group —Wisconsin's tiny band of zealous Trotskyites . . . joined by a perfectly weird medley of the other protest groupies who invariably show up when storms brew in Indian Country."[24]

Predictably, Clifton's efforts to be non-partisan led conservatives to accuse him of aiding Communist Indians, liberals to reject him for failing to turn over all funds to approved groups, and one costumed (tragically, in the garb of a distant and alien southwestern tribe), pistol-toting Warrior to threaten him with death. Lost in these factional and theatrical machinations, of course, were whatever common desires and needs might have remained among the tribal people themselves.

This regrettable experience shows the political manipulation to which contemporary Indian claims are routinely subjected, and also bears witness to the variety of native reactions to white presence. While a vague Pan-Indian agenda might be said to exist as a result of overwhelming white pressure, it is not as easily identifiable as some might think. The most radical agenda should certainly not to be accepted as representing the true and only "Indian" voice.

Quite clearly, Indian issues are now as much enmeshed in power politics as they are in the pursuit of justice. Government policy towards Native Americans has long involved large questions of history and philosophy, which engaged everyone from religious and political idealists to commercial opportunists and ideologues.[25] Different views have gotten the upper hand at different times, but currently native views—at least of a certain kind—

serve as a trump card over all others. No matter how native views may vary, only the high-minded Native Americans imagined by the Berkeley City Council—rather than, say, their lowly relations in profit-minded tribes permitting reservation gambling casinos —are allowed in elite circles legitimately to claim the name Native American. Clifton writes of the typical organization concerned with Indians today: "To meetings of these now come churchmen, statesmen, feminists, environmental activists, and academics—as suppliants, soliciting coalitions, seeking favors, checking their approval ratings."[26] We can easily picture the effects this atmosphere has produced on campuses and in publishing houses.

Multitudinously American

Questions about Native Americans' status in modern society in fact reflect a much more complicated set of issues now troubling the United States in particular and the Western world in general. The very terms we have begun to use to describe ourselves suggest widespread uncertainty. Back before the fall of the Berlin Wall, Marxists used to refer to the modern West as late-industrial or late-capitalist. With the demise of Marxism and socialism themselves as viable theories, other labels have become more prominent: post-Enlightenment, post-bourgeois, and—most inclusive of all—postmodern. It is in this intellectual and social environment that the repercussions of the 1492 controversy are felt most profoundly. The more extreme activists ostensibly serving the Native American cause often dismiss proposals for reparation, recognition, and reform in favor of profound rejection of, and revolution against, contemporary American life. They seem to use the label Native American only as a means of achieving goals having little or nothing to do with traditional native interests and probable futures.

Life in modern industrialized societies with pluralistic rather than monolithic cultures has raised fundamental questions about our relations to nature and to one another. At one time it was assumed that the outcome of modernization was inevitable. The sociologist Max Weber spoke of the "iron cage of modernity" in which traditional bonds would be summarily broken and individual belief, behavior, and social ties would be radically rationalized. But events late in the twentieth century have revealed that the iron cage is a sociological fiction. Modern societies, for all their standardizing and uniformizing tendencies, have not destroyed ethnic, religious, or familial identities. The totalitarian power of the former Communist societies was unable to stamp out such deep human loyalties, which survived and emerged with renewed force after those systems collapsed.

Clearer still, however, is the growth of a pervasive sentiment that insists these loyalties *not be allowed* to disappear. It is important to note the precise role that these natural human institutions are being asked to play. Unity amid particularity is now our global native condition, and, logically, a recalibration of the time-tested *e pluribus unum* should be our goal. But in the conditions of late modernity, radicals who see no good in modern economics, politics, or culture will not, of course, be satisfied with this traditional vision, no matter how it is extended to new groups. As Jacques Barzun has noted:

> Today the full realization of the Western world's practical concerns would not reconcile and make happy its chief denouncers. It might make the poor and disfranchised happier, but one may wonder for how long, since those already free from want, tyranny, ignorance, and superstition declare themselves the most oppressed and miserable of men and willingly risk what they have in order to smash the system.[27]

The postmodern disenchantment runs deep, even with those things that would formerly have been considered indisputable, precious, and historically unique achievements. Again Barzun: "Like representative government, like capitalism, like traditional religion, the culture that the West has been painstakingly fashioning since Columbus has ceased to serve and satisfy."[28]

One response to this situation—a response traced in detail in the preceding chapters—is to seek to escape to some non-European age before and untouched by Columbus, because our Western legacy is held, usually on scant acquaintance, to be responsible for all our present miseries. Native cultures, largely unknown, have the advantage of at least never having exerted much influence on our societies. In desperation some people regard the neolithic inhabitants of the pre-contact Americas as a potential *deus ex machina*, a deliverer from the world we have created for ourselves.

But this solution comes at a high price and not only to those who benefit from the current arrangements. It places an enormous burden on native groups, who are not allowed simply to become a more respected voice in the American mosaic. They must redefine the whole set of human relations with other humans and with the natural world. Unfairly, living Native Americans are made to choose between assimilation to the mainstream culture and symbolic death, on the one hand, and separation and marginality for the foreseeable future, on the other. Unlike other ethnic peoples on these shores, Native Americans are considered most authentically themselves only when they live as they did five hundred years ago.

This inflexibility may advance certain agendas within the mainstream culture, but it is of questionable value to Native Americans. For those who seek the good of both Native Americans and modern culture as a whole, the best relationship—barring some fresh currents of thought on our way toward a new epoch in world history—can only be something of a dialectic. The mainstream culture will, without doubt, continue to dominate the development of native communities. But native communities are in a better position than at any time in their history to resist where they will and to make such contributions as they can to mainstream culture. The struggle is unequal, and native contributions will not go unopposed, and they may even be ignored. But in this they will be no different than German, Jewish, Italian, Polish, African, Hispanic, Korean, Vietnamese, and a host of other influences on American society.

The alternative is the ghetto. Any group may choose isolation as a means of retaining cultural purity, of course, but the inevitable

167

accompaniment of that choice is marginalization. A freely chosen condition cannot also then be a case of complaint and group claim against the rest of society. In our world such claims will simply not be heeded. If the past five hundred years of atrocities, openness, misunderstanding, freedom, and slavery have taught us anything, they should have taught us that the United States—more than any other society in history—has at least been willing to grapple with the pursuit of justice for a wide variety of peoples. That process is not complete, or perhaps even completable. But as millions around the world have demonstrated in recent years, the promises of American-style democracy and society offer greater hope for all peoples than any other known system.

One undeniable impulse behind the promotion of Indian culture under the aegis of redefining 1492 is a perceived lack of spirituality in modern life. Joseph Epes Brown describes the difference between our lives and those of Native Americans in which "religion"

> is not a separate category of activity or experience [but] is in complex interrelationships with all aspects of the peoples' lifeways. Shared principles underlie sacred concepts that are specific to each of nature's manifestations and also to what could be called sacred geography. In addition, a special understanding of language in which words constitute distinct units of sacred power. Sacred forms extend to architectural styles so that each dwelling . . . is an image of the cosmos. Mysticism, in its original and thus deepest sense, is an experiential reality within Native American spiritual traditions.[29]

As is clear from this quotation, however, the interest in Native American spirituality actually reflects a Western sense of discontinuity with the fullness of our own cultural background. The ideal describes something close to a Holy Roman Empire and its sacred social order, art, and architecture.

Much of the current revisionist agenda, properly understood, comes close to endorsing deep currents in the very mainstream European culture the multiculturalists abhor. When Robert Maynard Hutchins and Mortimer Adler were criticized for not including masterpieces from the East in their Great Books series, for example, they argued that they had to draw a limit to the volumes somewhere. But then they pointed out—quite rightly—that the works many people suggested for inclusion (out of a kind of proto-multiculturalism) were far more similar to ancient and medieval European literature than their modern proponents might have suspected.[30] The same is true, *mutatis mutandis*, of the pitting of certain indigenous, or supposedly indigenous, cultural elements against the modern Western world. The protest is, in its most profound moments, a Western objection to the disappearance or attenuation of human riches within the West itself.

Native American culture may not have much to say directly to our current crises, but it may at least remind us of some essential things. It would be far better for us, better physically and better spiritually, to do Corn Dances or Rain Dances on Saturdays or Sundays than to spend so much time at shopping malls, for instance. A certain exuberance about nature and about the spiritual, properly understood, would open some windows in our climate-controlled world.

But perhaps the profoundest lesson we may hope to learn from contemplating 1492 is that it is important for every people to have a vigorous culture. A multiculturalist will admit this in every case save one, that of so-called Western culture. Like it or not, Western culture with its own particularities and its openness to light from the outside is the cultural matrix upon which the world has become, if not unified, then set on a path of something like universal mutual intercourse. No other culture in the world has—or probably could have—undertaken that task.

The Western tradition is debased, cut off from or in uncertain relation to its own roots. But those roots are what make an authentic multiculturalism possible at all. At its best, the West has integrated what is good and true into itself without losing its own momentum. As we look back at the last five hundred years of world history, we should be grateful that even today's poor excuse for Western culture—and not some monolithic political or theological system—presides over all our cultural futures as we approach the second millennium. Columbus succeeded in his vision of universal evangelization at least to that extent.

Life at the end of the twentieth century is in many of the deepest human ways hard, and sources of light seem few. Since the future is unknowable, we naturally turn to the civilizations of the past for enlightenment. When we do so, however, we must be ready to look honestly at the record. With respect to Native Americans, to do anything less is to practice the final imperialism: redefining the historical facts to fit our own categories. There are no perfect societies in America's or any other region's past, and any attempt to realize such a fiction is a flight both from truth and from responsibility.

Such flights are understandable. As anthropologists have discovered, primitive cultures prefer cyclical visions of nature and human life because they promise escape from the terrors, tragedies, and epic demands of history. In modern societies we have not entirely outgrown that impulse. An ominous feature of the more radical of such flights, however, is the sharp alienation from our common American culture that they represent. If Columbus was a wicked and rootless wanderer because he found no home in late-fifteenth-century Spain, what are we to say of his modern detractors who can find absolutely nothing good in their own science, technology, religion, social arrangements, and industry? Or to adapt an observation made by one of the primary creators of that bad Old World culture, if the critics cannot love their neighbors, whom they have seen, how can we rely on their love of the noble savage, whom they have not seen?

Notes

Introduction

1. Luigi Barzini, *The Europeans* (New York: Penguin Books, 1984), 11.
2. David W. Noble, *The Eternal Adam and the New World Garden* (New York: Grosset & Dunlap, 1968), ix.

Chapter One

1. Francisco López de Gómara, *Primera Parte de la Historia General de las Indias*, vol. 22 (Madrid: Biblioteca de Autores Españoles, 1852), 156.
2. Alfred W. Crosby, *The Columbian Exchange: Biological and Cultural Consequences of 1492* (Westport, Conn.: Greenwood Press, 1973); Henry F. Dobyns, *Their Number Become Thinned: Native American Population Dynamics in Eastern North America* (Knoxville: University of Tennessee Press, 1983); Edmundo O'Gorman, *The Invention of America: An Inquiry into the Historical Nature of the New World and the Meaning of Its History* (Bloomington: Indiana University Press, 1961). The theses of each of these volumes are discussed in following chapters of this book.
3. For example, Justin Winsor's *Christopher Columbus, and How He Received and Imparted the Spirit of Discovery* (Cambridge, Mass.: Cambridge University Press, 1891); and Henry Vignaud's later *Études critiques sur la vie de Christophe Colomb avant ses découvertes* (Paris: H. Welter, 1905).
4. For a brief overview of this history, see chapter 16, "His Place in History," in John Noble Wilford, *The Mysterious History of Columbus* (New York: Knopf, 1991).
5. On these figures see E. T. Dubois, "Léon Bloy, Paul Claudel, and the Revaluation of the Significance of Columbus," in *Currents of Thought in French Literature* (New York: Barnes & Noble, 1966), 131–44.
6. Leo XIII, *Quarto abeunte saeculo,* in *1878–1903*, vol. 2 of *The Papal Encyclicals*, ed. Claudia Carlen (Raleigh, N.C.: McGrath, 1981), 285–88.
7. Jeffrey Burton Russell, *Inventing the Flat Earth: Columbus and Modern Historians* (New York: Praeger, 1991).
8. Irving's biography was first published in two volumes by the Carey, Lea & Blanchard Co., Philadelphia, 1837. An accessible modern text has been edited by James W. Tuttleton (Boston: Twayne, 1987).
9. Few facts survive about the council appointed to look into Columbus's

enterprise that go back to anywhere near the date of the event; they cannot properly be used in anything like Washington Irving's interpretation. For a sober survey of the record, see Felipe Fernández-Armesto, *Columbus* (New York: Oxford University Press, 1991), especially 53–54.

10. Russell, *Inventing the Flat Earth*, 51. The original text is in John J. Anderson, *Popular History of the United States* (New York: Clark & Maynard, 1880), 19.

11. Joseph Chiari, *Christopher Columbus* (New York: Gordian, 1979); quoted in Russell, 3.

12. Samuel Eliot Morison, *Admiral of the Ocean Sea*, vol. 1 (Boston: Little, Brown & Co., 1942), 88–89.

13. Russell, *Inventing the Flat Earth*, 44.

14. Daniel Boorstin, *The Discoverers* (New York: Vintage, 1985), 100–113.

15. Ibid., 173.

16. Kirkpatrick Sale, *The Conquest of Paradise: Christopher Columbus and the Columbian Legacy* (New York: Knopf, 1990).

17. Quoted in the introductory film to the exhibition show at the Smithsonian Museum of Natural History, 1991.

18. SAIIC Promotional Mailing, 1991.

19. Arthur M. Schlesinger, Jr., "Four Days with Fidel: A Havana Diary," *New York Review of Books*, 26 March 1992, 26.

20. Public statement on Friday, 24 November 1989, in protest outside the Florida Museum of Natural History's exhibit "First Encounters: Spanish Explorations in the Caribbean and the United States, 1492–1570." Quoted in Jan Elliott, *Exhibiting Ideology* (A Review of "First Encounters") published by the Racial Justice Working Group, Prophetic Justice Unit of the National Council of Churches of Christ in the USA, New York, 1990.

21. J. Carter Brown, "Foreword," in *Circa 1492: Art in the Age of Exploration*, ed. Jay A. Levenson (Washington: National Gallery of Art, 1991), 9.

22. National Council of Churches in the USA, *A Faithful Response to the 500th Anniversary of the Arrival of Christopher Columbus* (Resolution adopted by the Governing Board 17 May 1990), 475 Riverside Drive, New York, N.Y.

23. National Conference of Catholic Bishops (U.S.), "Heritage and Hope: Evangelization in America" (Pastoral letter), *Origins* 20 (6 December 1990): 415.

24. Demetria Martinez, "Bishop Challenges Knights To Drop Columbus," *National Catholic Reporter*, 25 August 1991.

25. Quoted by Charles Krauthammer, "Hail Columbus, Dead White Male," *Time*, 27 May 1991, 74.

26. Hans Koning, "Don't Celebrate 1492—Mourn It," *New York Times*, 14 August 1990.

27. Alvin P. Sanoff, "The Myths of Columbus" (Interview with Kirkpatrick Sale), *U.S. News & World Report*, 8 October 1990, 74.

28. Sale, *Conquest of Paradise*, 160.

29. Ibid., 74.

30. Ibid., 82.

31. Ibid., 125.

32. Ibid., 113.

33. Ibid., 369.

34. David Marbury-Lewis, "Millennium: Tribal Wisdom and the Modern World," PBS, 11 May 1992.

35. Stephen Thernstrom, "The Columbus Controversy," *The American Educator* 16, no. 1 (Spring 1992): 31.

36. John Leo, "P.C. Follies," *U.S. News & World Report*, 27 January 1992, 26.

37. William D. Phillips, Jr., and Carla Rahn Phillips, *The Worlds of Christopher Columbus* (New York: Cambridge University Press, 1992), 7.

CHAPTER TWO

1. C. Varela, ed., *Cristóbal Colón, Textos y documentos completos* (Madrid: 1984), 323–24. A more literal but less clear translation, along with the original Spanish text, may be found in vol. 2 of Cecil Jane., ed., *The Four Voyages of Columbus*, reprint (New York: Dover, 1988), 94–95.

2. Jane, *Four Voyages*, xxviii–xxix.

3. Fernández-Armesto, *Columbus*. A more introductory, well-balanced study is Phillips and Phillips, *Worlds of Christopher Columbus*.

4. A good short survey of the little that we possess about Cabot is presented in chapter 6, "John Cabot's Voyages," in Samuel Eliot Morison, *The European Discovery of America: The Northern Voyages* (New York: Oxford University Press, 1971).

5. Morison, *Admiral of the Ocean Sea*, vol. 2, 164.

6. Bartolomé de Las Casas, *Historia de las Indias*, vol. 1 (Mexico City: Fondo de cultura económica, 1951), 466 (author's translation).

7. Bartolomé de Las Casas, *History of the Indies*, trans. and ed. Andrée Collard (New York: Harper & Row, 1971), 53.

8. Paolo Emilio Taviani, *Columbus, The Great Adventure*, trans. Luciano F. Farina and Marc A. Beckwith (New York: Orion Books, 1991), 102.

9. On this point and for an exhaustive and exhausting analysis of the *Log*, see David Henige, *In Search of Columbus: The Sources for the First Voyage* (Tucson: University of Arizona Press, 1991). As Henige's dedication of this volume to Pierre Bayle and a legion of other details show, skepticism may become as confining a dogma as credulousness.

10. Christopher Columbus, *The Log of Christopher Columbus*, trans. Robert H. Fuson (Camden, Maine: International Marine Publishing, 1992), 32. See also Oliver Dunn and James E. Kelley, Jr.'s translation (Norman: University of Oklahoma Press, 1989).

11. "Teach the Truth About Columbus," *Washington Post*, 3 September 1991.

12. An early historian, Andrés Bernáldez, recounts a similar request by another cacique on Jamaica during the second voyage. See Jane, *Four Voyages*, vol. 1, 164.

13. Wilford, *Mysterious History*, 170.

14. Jane, *Four Voyages*, vol. 1., 88.

15. Felipe Fernández-Armesto, "In Defense of Columbus: The Trouble With Eden," *The Economist*, 21 December 1991–3 January 1992, 74.

16. Morison, *Admiral of the Ocean Sea*, vol. 2, 90.

17. Fernández-Armesto, *Columbus*, 112.

18. Quoted in Morison, *Admiral of the Ocean Sea*, vol. 2, 304.

19. Fernández-Armesto, *Columbus*, 122.

173

20. Phillips and Phillips, *Worlds of Christopher Columbus*, 90.

21. Jane, *Four Voyages*, vol. 2., 66.

22. See chapter 7, "The Ball Game," in Eugenio Fernández Méndez, *Art and Mythology of the Taíno Indians of the Greater West Indies* (San Juan: Ediciones "El Cemi," 1972), 62.

23. Ibid., 61–69.

24. Jane, *Four Voyages*, vol. 1, 94.

25. Wilford, *Mysterious History*, 173.

26. The exact site of landfall continues to be hotly disputed and will likely remain so barring some conclusive archeological discovery. San Salvador, formerly Watlings Island under British rule, is the most popular candidate with Samana Cay in the next place. Other sites have been suggested because they show convincing geographical features. Robert Fuson gives a handy list of the candidates, their major sponsors, and the dates they have been proposed in the introduction to his translation of *The Log of Christopher Columbus*. The inconclusiveness of this dispute mirrors the indeterminable nature of many questions relating to the voyages.

27. Phillips and Phillips, *Worlds of Christopher Columbus*, 79.

28. F. W. Mote, "China in the Age of Columbus," in *Circa 1492,* ed. Levenson, 337–50.

29. Wilford, *Mysterious History*, 7.

30. "Introductory Letter," in Christopher Columbus, *Libro de las profecías*, trans. and ed. Delno C. West and August Kling (Gainesville: University of Florida Press, 1991), 105.

31. Ibid., 111.

32. Fernández-Armesto, *Columbus*, passim.

33. Samuel Eliot Morison, for example, gives the *Libro de las profecías* only three passing references in the two large volumes of *Admiral of the Ocean Sea*.

34. Cf. Sale, *Conquest of Paradise*, 188–91.

35. Cristóbal Colón, *Libro de las profecías*, trans. and ed. F. Morales Pedrón (Madrid: Colleción Tabula Americae, 1984).

36. "Introduction," in Columbus, *Libro de las profecías*, 4.

37. Ibid., 74–75.

38. Several recent biographers accept this diagnosis on the basis of G. Weissmann, *They All Laughed at Christopher Columbus: Tales of Medicine and the Art of Discovery* (New York: Times Books, 1987).

39. Columbus, *Libro de las profecías*, 86.

40. Leonard I. Sweet, "Christopher Columbus and the Millennial Vision of the New World," *The Catholic Historical Review* 72, no. 3 (July 1986): 381. See also Marcel Bataillon, "The Idea of the Discovery of America Among the Spaniards of the Sixteenth Century," in *Spain in the Fifteenth Century: 1369-1516*, ed. Roger Highfield (New York: Harper & Row, 1972), 453.

41. Sweet, "Millennial Vision," 378.

42. Felipe Fernández-Armesto, *Ferdinand and Isabella* (New York: Taplinger, 1975), 132–33.

43. T. S. Eliot, *Collected Poems, 1909–1935* (New York: Harcourt, Brace & World, 1962), 110.

44. Sweet, "Millennial Vision," 381.
45. Columbus, *Libro de las profecías*, 107.
46. See Sale, *Conquest of Paradise*, among others.
47. Columbus, *The Log*, 115, 117, 132, 138, and 154 for Columbus's initial doubts. Quotation in text from 132.
48. Phillips and Phillips, *Worlds*, 295, n. 22.
49. Columbus, *The Log*, 172.
50. Las Casas, *Historia de las Indias*, vol. 1, 30–31 (author's translation).
51. Columbus, *Libro de las profecías*, 258–59.
52. One scholar (Taviani, *Columbus*, 263), however, placing yet another symbolic load on Columbus, has argued that he embodies "the creative genius of Italy shaping the beginning of the modern age." Columbus's pivotal position on the way toward the modern world perhaps makes such terminological tugs of war inevitable.
53. J. R. S. Phillips, *Medieval Expansion of Europe* (New York: Oxford University Press, 1988), 255.
54. Tzvetan Todorov, *The Conquest of America: The Question of the Other*, trans. Richard Howard (New York: Harper & Row, 1985), 84.
55. Stephen Greenblatt, *Marvelous Possessions: The Wonder of the New World* (Chicago: University of Chicago Press, 1991), 24.
56. Ibid., 71.
57. Ibid., 58, 70.
58. Anthony Burgess, *On Mozart: A Paean for Wolfgang* (New York: Ticknor & Fields, 1991).
59. "Myths of Columbus," 74.
60. Simón Bolívar, *Selected Writings*, ed. Harold A. Bierck, Jr., vol. 1 (New York: Colonial Press, 1951), 119, quoted in Lewis Hanke, *Aristotle and the American Indians: A Study in Race Prejudice in the Modern World* (Bloomington: Indiana University Press, 1975), 114.

CHAPTER THREE

1. Francis Parkman, *The Jesuits in North America*, in vol. 1 of *Parkman: France and England in North American* (New York: Library of America, 1983), 432.
2. For both legends see Charles Gibson, *The Black Legend: Anti-Spanish Attitudes in the Old World and the New* (New York: Knopf, 1971).
3. Parkman, *Jesuits in North America*, 623.
4. G. K. Chesterton, "*Illustrated London News*, 23 April 1927," in vol. 34 of *Collected Works* (San Francisco: Ignatius Press, 1986).
5. Some Catholic bishops in Latin America have argued that Protestant groups have been especially active in perpetuating stereotypes about early Catholic missions in the New World. In 1991 Cardinal Nicolas de Jesus López Rodriques, president of the Latin American Bishops Conference, remarked on the lack of rancor indigenous peoples manifest towards the Church in all opinion surveys that have been conducted. He also designated "growing reform protestantism as being one of the principal interested parties to oppose itself to the presence of the Catholic Church in the Americas." Quoted in *Liaisons Latino-*

Americaines, no. 86 (Paris, novembre 1991). While both the cardinal's contentions may be somewhat exaggerated, these matters rarely appear in contemporary discussions of 1492 and after.

6. National Council of Churches, *A Faithful Response*.

7. Stafford Poole, "Iberian Catholicism Comes to the Americas," in *Christianity Comes to the Americas*, ed. Stafford Poole, Charles H. Lippy, and Robert Choquette (New York: Giniger Books, 1992), 125–26.

8. Gary Nash, *Red, White, and Black: The Peoples of Early America* (Englewood Cliffs, N.J.: Prentice-Hall, 1974), 62–63.

9. J. H. Elliott, *Imperial Spain, 1469–1710* (New York: Penguin Books, 1963), 70. Elliott is also a very useful guide to other facts needed to assess moral issues raised by New World contacts.

10. See in particular Mario Paredes, "A Hispanic Reaction to the NCC," Northeast Hispanic Catholic Center, 1011 First Avenue, New York, New York, 25 July 1991. Reprinted in *Origins* 20 (16 August 1990): 173–74.

11. James Muldoon, "The Columbus Quincentennial: Should Christians Celebrate It?", *America*, 27 October 1990, 300.

12. Quoted in Poole, "Iberian Catholicism," 79.

13. Quoted in Lewis Hanke, *All Mankind Is One: A Study of the Disputation Between Bartolomé de las Casas and Juan Ginés Sepúlveda in 1550 on the Intellectual and Religious Capacity of the American Indians* (DeKalb: Northern Illinois University Press, 1974), 7.

14. Ibid., 8.

15. A long excerpt from Mendoza's *relación de mando* (report to his replacement) may be found in Woodrow W. Borah, *Justice by Insurance: The General Indian Court of Colonial Mexico and the Legal Aides of the Half-Real* (Berkeley: University of California Press, 1983), 66–67. For Mendoza's kind but realistic assessment of the Indians, see A. S. Aiton, *Antonio de Mendoza: First Viceroy of New Spain* (New York: Russell & Russell, 1927), 94.

16. Hanke, *All Mankind Is One*, 16.

17. Among many other instances, Parkman cites, for example, the martyr Jean de Brébeuf's letter to the General of the Jesuits: "*Ce qu'il faut demander, avant tout, des ouvriers destinés á cette mission, c'est une douceur et une patience à toute épreuve*" (*Jesuits in North America*, 494).

18. Though for a long time only a few chapters of this work were known to have survived, a reconstructed text has been produced in the series *The Classics of Western Spirituality* (New York: Paulist Press, 1992).

19. Hanke, *All Mankind Is One*, xi.

20. Poole, "Iberian Catholicism," 87.

21. W. Arens, *The Man-Eating Myth: Anthropology and Anthropophagy* (New York: Oxford University Press, 1979).

22. Leslie Bethell, ed., *The Cambridge History of Latin America*, vol. 1 (New York: Cambridge University Press, 1984), 272.

23. Poole, "Iberian Catholicism," 87.

24. See Ramón Menéndez Pidal, *El Padre Las Casas. Su doble personalidad* (Madrid: Espasa Calpe, 1963).

25. ". . . *aunque eran crueles, pero eran menudas, sotiles y exquisitas . . . .*" Silva Tena also remarks that the phrase would have been envied by Octave Mirabeau and the Marquis de Sade, in "El Sacrificio Humano En La *Apologética Historia*," *Historia Mexicana* 16 (1967): 349.

26. Hanke, *All Mankind Is One,* 27.

27. Sale, *Conquest of Paradise,* 134.

28. The material on Vitoria is surprisingly small for such a pivotal figure, reflecting some historical myopia. A substantial portion of his work with commentary has been edited recently by Anthony Padgen and Jeremy Lawrence, *Vitoria, Political Writings* (New York: Cambridge University Press, 1991). The passages cited here are taken from selections from Vitoria's work jointly published by the University of Salamanca and the Catholic University of America in Spanish and English for the quincentenary as *The Rights and Obligations of Indians and Spaniards in the New World,* ed. Luciano Pereña Vicente (Salamanca and Washington, 1991).

29. Vitoria, *Rights and Obligations,* 17–19.

30. Ibid., 23, 29.

31. Ibid., 23.

32. Ibid., 31.

33. James Brown Scott, *The Spanish Origin of International Law* (Washington: Georgetown University Press, 1928), 21.

34. Ibid., 22.

35. Poole, "Iberian Catholicism," 84.

36. James Boswell, *Life of Johnson,* ed. George Birbeck Hill, revised by L. F. Powell, vol. 1 (Oxford: Oxford University Press, 1934), 455.

37. See Parkman, *Jesuits in North America*; and especially James T. Moore, *Indian and Jesuit: A Seventeenth-Century Encounter* (Chicago: Loyola University Press, 1982).

38. Reuben Gold Thwaite edited these in *The Jesuit Relations and Allied Documents,* 73 vols. (Cleveland: Burrows Brothers, 1896–1901). A good selection from this massive record is Edna Kenton, ed., *The Jesuit Relations and Allied Documents* (New York: A. Boni and C. Boni, 1925).

39. This material was presented by Bernard Knox in his 1992 Jefferson Lecture "The Oldest Dead White European Males," reprinted in *The New Republic,* 25 May 1992, 27–36.

40. Parkman, *Jesuits in North America,* 670–71.

41. See Louis C. Faron, "A Continent On The Move," in *America in 1492: The World of the Indian Peoples Before the Arrival of Columbus,* ed. Alvin M. Josephy, Jr. (New York: Knopf, 1992), 177–214. Although Josephy clearly intended to weigh in on the indigenous side in the 1992 debate, his aims are not always supported by the contributors to this volume.

42. Quoted in Catherine L. Albanese, *Nature Religion in America: From the Algonkian Indians to the New Age* (Chicago: University of Chicago Press, 1990), 35.

43. William Kellaway, *The New England Company, 1649–1776: Missionary Society to the American Indian* (London: Longmans, 1961), 109.

44. Mario Vargas Llosa, "Questions of Conquest," *Harper's*, December 1990, 51.

CHAPTER FOUR

1. Arthur M. Schlesinger, Jr., *The Disuniting of America: Reflections on a Multicultural Society* (New York: W. W. Norton, 1992), 127.

2. Åke Hultkrantz, *Native Religions of North America* (San Francisco: Harper & Row, 1987), 24.

3. Åke Hultkrantz, *Belief and Worship in Native North America*, ed. Christopher Vecsey (Syracuse, N.Y.: Syracuse University Press, 1981), 125.

4. Ibid.

5. Ibid., 129.

6. William N. Fenton, "Northern Iroquoian Culture Patterns," in vol. 15 of *Handbook of North American Indians*, ed. Bruce G. Trigger (Washington: Smithsonian Institution Press, 1978), 298.

7. Ibid., 302.

8. For a sympathetic but reliable guide to the current state of knowledge about the Mayas, see Linda Schele and David Freidel, *A Forest of Kings: The Untold Story of the Ancient Maya* (New York: William Morrow, 1990).

9. This way of reading Genesis is clearly tendentious, but a powerful temptation. Even as fair a man as Albert Camus, who though not a Christian was generally fair to Christianity, argued in *The Rebel*, "For the Christian, as for the Marxist, nature must be subdued. The Greeks are of the opinion that it is better to obey it. The love of the ancients for the cosmos was completely unknown to the first Christians" (New York: Vintage Books, 1956, 190). This is mistaken in several ways, but deserves some attention as an indication of how easy it is to identify incorrectly modern industrialism with the deep Judeo-Christian roots of Western culture.

10. Jacques Soustelle, *Daily Life of the Aztecs on the Eve of the Spanish Conquest*, trans. Patrick O'Brien (Palo Alto: Stanford University Press, 1970), 101–2.

11. English translation with original Spanish in *Collected Poems, 1957–1987* (New York: New Directions, 1987).

12. This passage and some of the points that follow are drawn from Paz's essay "Reflexiones de un intruso," in the magazine he edits, *Vuelta*, January 1987, 20–26 (author's translation). Paz's appraisal is consistent with that of one of the premier scholars of Aztec life, Jacques Soustelle, who has written, "Perhaps no people in history has been as much haunted by the grim presence of death as the [ancient] Mexicans."

13. Davíd Carrasco, *Religions of Mesoamerica* (San Francisco: Harper and Row, 1990).

14. Mircea Eliade, *Cosmos and History: The Myth of the Eternal Return* (New York: Harper Torchbooks, 1959).

15. The present writer once made these arguments to a class at the U.S. Foreign Service Institute. One of the students, echoing what he had heard in other forums about minority issues, replied that the Indian culture "worked for them." This is in a sense true, just as the enslavement of the Israelites "worked"

178

for the ancient Egyptians. Anthropological neutrality and a humanitarian belief in the value of all cultures—valid enough within limits—cannot replace our necessary judgment of what should and should not be permitted in civilized society. A sentimental belief in the equal dignity of all cultures leads inevitably, in the practical sphere, to defense of sacrificial murder.

16. Paz, "Reflexiones de un intruso."

17. Bernal Diaz del Castillo, *History of New Spain*, trans. and ed. J. M. Cohen (New York: Penguin Books, 1983) is the most easily available translation. Cohen has condensed some passages and deleted others, somewhat distorting the text. The translation quoted here is the full English version by Maurice Keating (New York: National Travel Club, 1927), xxv.

18. Diaz del Castillo, *History of New Spain*, trans. Keating, 105.

19. Peter Iverson, "Taking Care of the Earth and Sky," in *America in 1492*, ed. Josephy, 96.

20. Because descriptions of these kinds of rituals become bogged down in explanatory digressions in many analyses, the reader seeking an introduction to this material would do best to turn to a popular but competent general guide such as James A. Maxwell, ed., *America's Fascinating Indian Heritage* (Pleasantville, N.Y.: Reader's Digest Association, 1978) before going on to more detailed studies.

21. See "On Campus," *New York Times*, 20 October 1991.

22. For a sophisticated discussion of this phenomena, see Alice B. Kehoe, "Primal Gaia: Primitivists and Plastic Medicine Men," in *The Invented Indian: Cultural Fictions and Government Policies*, ed. James B. Clifton (New Brunswick, N.J.: Transaction Books, 1990), 193–210.

23. Kim Masters, "Some Might Call It Art. . . ," *Washington Post*, 9 February 1992, G10.

24. Samuel Eliot Morison, ed. and trans., *Journals and Other Documents on the Life and Voyages of Christopher Columbus* (New York: Heritage, 1963), 212.

25. Though hotly contested by revisionists, no convincing evidence has emerged to discredit the general lines of this history. See Alvin M. Josephy, *The Indian Heritage of America* (New York: Bantam, 1968), 264–65.

26. See Jay Miller, "A Kinship of Spirit," in *America in 1492*, ed. Josephy, 309.

27. For some of the recent literary manifestations of this rereading, see Garry Wills's comments on Aimé Cesaire's play *Une tempête* and revisionist productions of Shakespeare in "Goodbye, Columbus," *New York Review of Books*, 22 November 1990, 6–7.

28. Thomas More, *Utopia*, trans. Paul Turner (New York: Penguin, 1961), 30–31.

29. J. H. Elliott, "A World United," in *Circa 1492*, ed. Levenson, 650.

30. Ibid.

31. Sale, *Conquest of Paradise*, 58.

32. George Holmes, ed., *Oxford Illustrated History of Medieval Europe* (New York: Oxford University Press, 1990), 354.

33. John R. Hale, *Age of Exploration* (New York: Time Inc., 1967), 16–17.

34. Peter Denley, "The Mediterranean in the Age of the Renaissance," in *Oxford Illustrated History*, ed. Holmes, 243.

35. Sale, *Conquest of Paradise*, 37.

36. Ibid., 18.

37. Sam Gill, *Native American Religions: An Introduction* (Belmont, Cal.: Wadsworth, 1982), 22.

38. Holmes, *Oxford Illustrated History*, 352.

39. Francis Bacon, *The Advancement of Learning*, vol. 1 of *Francis Bacon*, ed. Arthur Johnston (New York: Schocken, 1965), 44.

40. Gill, *Native American Religions*, 22.

41. Edmundo O'Gorman, *Invention of America*.

42. This entire anecdote may be found in Francis Parkman, *La Salle and the Discovery of the Great West*, in vol. 1 of *Parkman: France and England in North America*, 725–26.

CHAPTER FIVE

1. 1992/Kairos USA describes itself as "a partnership movement of local and national groups and churches" whose contact person is at the National Council of Churches headquarters, 475 Riverside Drive, New York, N.Y. The statement was reprinted in *Sojourners* magazine, vol. 20, no. 8 (October 1991): 27.

2. Cited by Steven King and Liliana Campos Dudley, "Nature's Future," in *Seeds of Change: Five Hundred Years Since Columbus*, ed. Herman J. Viola and Carolyn Margolis (Washington: Smithsonian Institution Press, 1991).

3. See Winona LaDuke, "We Are Still Here," *Sojourners* 20, no. 8 (October 1991): 16.

4. Viola and Margolis, *Seeds of Change*, 9.

5. Ibid., 12.

6. Kenneth Maxwell has traced these connections in two long articles: "The Tragedy of the Amazon," *New York Review of Books*, 7 March 1991; and "The Mystery of Chico Mendes," *New York Review of Books*, 28 March 1991.

7. Brown, "Foreword," in *Circa 1492*, ed. Levenson, 9.

8. Levenson, *Circa 1492*, 19.

9. Simon Schama, "They All Laughed at Christopher Columbus," *The New Republic*, 6–13 January 1992, 33.

10. Bill McAllister, "Columbus Jubilee Panel Gets Few Answers," *Washington Post*, 22 November 1991, A23.

11. Wills, "Goodbye, Columbus," 6.

12. Louis De Vorsey, Jr., *Keys to the Encounter: A Library of Congress Resource Guide for the Study of the Age of Discovery* (Washington: Library of Congress, 1991).

13. Ibid., vii.

14. In a television debate with the author, C-Span II, "Close Up America," 5 July 1991.

15. Raymond Sokolov, *Why We Eat What We Eat* (New York: Summit Books, 1992), 15–16.

16. Raymond Sokolov, "Stop Knocking Columbus," *Newsweek*, Special Issue, Fall/Winter 1991, 82.

17. *National Geographic* 180, no. 4 (October 1991): 53.

18. Peter Steinfels, "Beliefs," *New York Times*, 26 October 1991, A25.

19. Vincent Canby, "Saving the Huron Indians: A Disaster for Both Sides" (Review of *Black Robe*), *New York Times*, 30 October 1991, C15.

20. Joel W. Martin, *Sacred Revolt: The Muskogees Struggle for a New World* (Boston: Beacon Press, 1991).

21. Reported in *The Chronicle of Higher Education*, 11 March 1992, A16.

22. Peter Nabokov and Dean Snow, "Farmers of the Woodlands," in *American in 1492*, ed. Josephy, 140–41. Nabokov and Stone follow the usual North American practice of denying that human sacrifice could have been indigenous to North American Indians: "Along with some other Caddoan- and Muskogean-speaking groups of the Gulf Coast region, the Natchez practiced human sacrifice—more evidence of the diffusion of Mexican traits into their territories." Evidence of sacrifice we have; evidence of diffusion from another culture is another matter and has to be demonstrated, not posited.

23. *Scholastic Update* 125, no. 2, September 1991.

24. The document was "developed by the National Council for the Social Studies, October 1991." Co-signatories include organizations like the American Anthropological Association, National Education Association, and World History Association.

25. A film about Columbus was scheduled for release in 1992 but appeared too late to be used in this chapter. Early signs of what it is likely to be were forthcoming. Though described as being non-political, it was directed by the same person who directed the violent feminist film *Thelma and Louise*, a story of two young women who hit the road and casually kill and assault offensive men. In the 1992 *Columbus*, Marlon Brando was scheduled to play the inquisitor Torquemada, a colorful role but not a figure who had much to do with the history of the New World. Another film was also planned.

CHAPTER SIX

1. *The Daily Californian*, 14 January 1992.

2. Timothy Egan, "Chief's 1854 Lament Linked to Ecological Script of 1971," *New York Times*, 21 April 1992, A1, A17.

3. Daniel T. Reff, "Anthropological Analysis of Exploration Texts: Cultural Discourse and the Ethnological Import of Fray Marcos de Niza's Journey to Cibola," *The American Anthropologist*, no. 93 (September 1991).

4. Maxwell, *America's Fascinating Indian Heritage*, 283.

5. Quoted in Elisabeth Tooker, "The United States Constitution and the Iroquois League," in *Invented Indian*, ed. Clifton. Tooker's entire essay is a valuable review of the claims and counterclaims.

6. Schlesinger, *Disuniting of America*, 97

7. Francis Jennings, *The Ambiguous Iroquois Empire: The Covenant Chain of Indian Tribes with English Colonies from Its Beginning to the Lancaster Treaty of 1744* (New York: W. W. Norton, 1984), 94.

8. Ibid., 25.

9. Miguel León-Portilla, "Men of Maize," in *America in 1492*, ed. Josephy, 153.

10. Sale, *Conquest of Paradise*, 98.

11. Nash, *Red, White, and Black*, 81.

12. See, for example, Anthony Pagden, *The Fall of Natural Man: The American Indian and the Origins of Comparative Ethnology* (Cambridge: Cambridge University Press, 1982).

13. See Robert Graves, *The Greek Myths*, vol. 1 (Middlesex: Penguin Books, 1964), 30, and ff. for similar creation stories.

14. Sam Gill, "Religious Forms and Themes," in *America in 1492*, ed. Josephy, 290.

15. Miller, "Kinship of Spirit," in *America in 1492*, ed. Josephy, 327.

16. Ibid., 337.

17. Ibid., 321.

18. On these issues and many other details, see T. J. Brasser, "Early Indian-European Contacts," in vol. 15 of *Handbook of North American Indians*, ed. Trigger, 78–88.

19. Ibid., 84.

20. Russell Bourne, *The Red King's Rebellion: Racial Politics in New England 1675–1678* (New York: Oxford University Press, 1990), xii.

21. Wilcomb E. Washburn, "Seventeenth-Century Indian Wars," in vol. 15 of *Handbook of North American Indians*, ed. Trigger, 99.

22. See in particular Clifton, "Introduction: Memoir, Exegesis," in *Invented Indian*.

23. Ibid., 5.

24. Ibid., 8.

25. See Francis Paul Prucha, *The Great Father: The United States Government and the American Indians*, 2 vols. (Lincoln: University of Nebraska Press, 1984); and Wilcomb E. Washburn, "History of Indian-White Relations," in vol. 4 of *Handbook of North American Indians*, ed. Trigger.

26. Clifton, "Introduction," in *Invented Indian*, 16.

27. Jacques Barzun, *The Culture We Deserve* (Middletown, Conn.: Wesleyan University Press, 1989), 175.

28. Ibid., 173.

29. Quoted in Kehoe, "Primal Gaia," in *Invented Indian*, ed. Clifton, 197–98.

30. Robert Maynard Hutchins and Mortimer Adler, eds., "East and West," in *The Great Conversation*, vol. 1. of *Great Books of the Western World* (Chicago: Encyclopedia Britannica, 1952), particularly 70–71.

Selected Bibliography

Aiton, A. S. *Antonio de Mendoza: First Viceroy of New Spain*. New York: Russell & Russell, 1927.

Albanese, Catherine L. *Nature Religion in America: From the Algonkian Indians to the New Age*. Chicago: University of Chicago Press, 1990.

Anawalt, Patricia Rieff, and Frances F. Berdan. "The Codex Mendoza." *Scientific American*, June 1992.

Anderson, John J. *Popular History of the United States*. New York: Clark & Maynard, 1880.

Arens, W. *The Man-Eating Myth: Anthropology and Anthropophagy*. New York: Oxford University Press, 1979.

Axtell, James. *The Invasion Within: The Contest of Cultures in Colonial North America*. New York: Oxford University Press, 1985.

Bacon, Francis. *Francis Bacon*. Edited by Arthur Johnston. New York: Schocken, 1965.

Barzini, Luigi. *The Europeans*. New York: Penguin Books, 1984.

Barzun, Jacques. *The Culture We Deserve*. Middletown, Conn.: Wesleyan University Press, 1989.

Bataillon, Marcel. "The Idea of the Discovery of America Among the Spaniards of the Sixteenth Century." In *Spain in the Fifteenth Century*, edited by Roger Highfield. New York: Harper & Row, 1972.

Bethell, Leslie, ed. *The Cambridge History of Latin America*. New York: Cambridge University Press, 1984.

Bolívar, Simón. *Selected Writings*. Edited by Harold A. Bierck, Jr. New York: Colonial Press, 1951.

Boorstin, Daniel. *The Discoverers*. New York: Vintage, 1985.

Borah, Woodrow W. *Justice by Insurance: The General Indian Court of Colonial Mexico and the Legal Aides of the Half-Real*. Berkeley: University of California Press, 1983.

Bourne, Russell. *The Red King's Rebellion: Racial Politics in New England 1675–1678*. New York: Oxford University Press, 1990.

Brasser, T. J. "Early Indian-European Contacts." In *Handbook of North American Indians*, edited by Bruce G. Trigger, vol. 15. Washington: Smithsonian Institution Press, 1978.

Brown, Joseph Epes. *The Spritual Legacy of the American Indian*. New York: Crossroad, 1982.

Canby, Vincent. "Saving the Huron Indians: A Disaster for Both Sides" (Review of *Black Robe*). *New York Times*, 30 October 1991.

Carrasco, Davíd. *Religions of Mesoamerica*. San Fancisco: Harper & Row, 1990.

Céspedes, Guillermo. *Latin America: The Early Years*. New York: Knopf, 1974.

Chesterton, G. K. "*Illustrated London News*, 23 April 1927." In *Collected Works*, vol 34. San Francisco: Ignatius, 1986.

Chiari, Joseph. *Christopher Columbus*. New York: Gordian, 1979.

Clifton, James B., ed. *The Invented Indian: Cultural Fictions and Government Policies*. New Brunswick, N.J.: Transaction Books, 1990.

Collins, John James. *Native American Religions: A Geographical Survey*. Native American Studies, vol. 1. Lewiston, Maine: Edwin Mueller Press, 1991.

Colón, Cristóbal. *Libro de las profecías*. Translated and edited by F. Morales Pedron. Madrid: Colleción Tabula Americae, 1984.

Columbus, Christopher. *Libro de las profecías*. Translated and edited by Delno C. West and August Kling. Gainesville: University of Florida Press, 1991.

——————. *The Log of Christopher Columbus*. Translated by Robert H. Fuson. Camden, Maine: International Marine Publishing, 1992.

Crosby, Alfred W. *The Columbian Exchange: Biological and Cultural Consequences of 1492*. Westport, Conn.: Greenwood Press, 1973.

The Daily Californian, 14 January 1992.

Davis, D. Dave. "Rumor of Cannibals." *Archeology* 45, no. 1 (January/February 1992).

de Lollis, C., et al., eds. *Raccolta di documenti e studi pubblicati dalla Reale Commisione Colombiana*. 14 vols. Rome: 1982–86.

De Vorsey, Louis, Jr. *Keys to the Encounter: A Library of Congress Resource Guide for the Study of the Age of Discovery*. Washington: Library of Congress, 1991.

Diaz del Castillo, Bernal. *History of New Spain*. Translated and edited by J. M. Cohen. New York: Penguin Books, 1983.

_____. *History of New Spain*. Translated by Maurice Keating. New York: National Travel Club, 1927.

Dobyns, Henry F. *Their Number Become Thinned: Native American Population Dynamics in Eastern North America*. Knoxville: University of Tennessee Press, 1983.

Dubois, E. T. "Léon Bloy, Paul Claudel, and the Revaluation of the Significance of Columbus." In *Currents of Thought in French Literature*. New York: Barnes & Noble, 1966.

Egan, Timothy. "Chief's 1854 Lament Linked to Ecological Script of 1971." *New York Times*, 21 April 1992.

Eliade, Mircea. *Cosmos and History: The Myth of the Eternal Return*. New York: Harper Torchbooks, 1959.

Elliott, Jan. *Exhibiting Ideology* (Review of "First Encounters"). Published by the Racial Justice Working Group, Prophetic Justice Unit of the National Council of the Churches of Christ in the U.S.A., New York, 1990.

Elliott, J. H. *Imperial Spain, 1469–1710*. New York: Penguin Books, 1963.

_____. *The Old World and the New, 1492–1650*. Cambridge: Cambridge University Press, 1970.

Fagan, Brian M. *Kingdoms of Gold, Kingdoms of Jade: The Americas Before Columbus*. London: Thames and Hudson, 1991.

Falcoff, Mark, "Was 1492 a Mistake?: Did Columbus Go Too Far?" *The American Enterprise* 3, no. 1 (January/February, 1992).

Fenton, William N. "Northern Iroquoian Culture Patterns." In *Handbook of North American Indians*, edited by Bruce G. Trigger, vol. 15. Washington: Smithsonian Institution Press, 1978.

Fernández-Armesto, Felipe, *Columbus*. New York: Oxford University Press, 1991.

_____. *Ferdinand and Isabella*. New York: Taplinger, 1975.

_____. "In Defence of Columbus: The Trouble With Eden." *The Economist*, 21 December 1991–3 January 1992.

Fernández Méndez, Eugenio. *Art and Mythology of the Taíno Indians of the Greater West Indies*. San Juan: Ediciones "El Cemi," 1972.

"1491: American Before Columbus." *National Geographic* 180, no. 4 (October 1991).

Geertz, Clifford. *The Interpretation of Cultures*. New York: Basic Books, 1973.

Gerace, Donald T., comp. *First San Salvador Conference: Columbus and His World*. San Salvador Island: Bahamian Field Station, 1987.

Gibson, Charles. *The Black Legend: Anti-Spanish Attitudes in the Old World and the New*. New York: Knopf, 1971.

Gill, Sam. *Native American Religions: An Introduction*. Belmont: Cal.: Wadsworth, 1982.

Graves, Robert. *The Greek Myths*. Middlesex: Penguin Books, 1964.

Greenblatt, Stephen. *Marvelous Possessions: The Wonder of the New World*. Chicago: University of Chicago Press, 1991.

Guier, Jorge Enrique. *Derecho precolombino*. San José, Costa Rica: Libro Libre, 1991.

Hale, John R. *The Age of Exploration*. New York: Time Inc., 1967.

――――――. *Renaissance Europe*. Berkeley: University of California Press, 1977.

Hanke, Lewis. *All Mankind Is One: A Study of the Disputation Between Bartolomé de las Casas and Juan Ginés Sepúlveda in 1550 on the Intellectual and Religious Capacity of the American Indians*. DeKalb: Northern Illinois University Press, 1974.

――――――. *Aristotle and the American Indians: A Study in Race Prejudice in the Modern World*. Bloomington: Indiana University Press, 1975.

――――――. *Bartolomé de las Casas, Historian*. Gainesville: University of Florida Press, 1952.

Henige, David. *In Search of Columbus: The Sources for the First Voyage*. Tucson: University of Arizona Press, 1991.

Highfield, Roger, ed. *Spain in the Fifteenth Century: 1369–1516*. New York: Harper & Row, 1972.

Highwater, Jamake. *The Primal Mind: Vision and Reality in Indian America*. New York: Harper & Row, 1981.

Holmes, George, ed. *Oxford Illustrated History of Medieval Europe*. New York: Oxford University Press, 1990.

Hultkrantz, Åke. *Belief and Worship in Native North America*. Edited by Christopher Vecsey. Syracuse, N.Y.: Syracuse University Press, 1981.

――――――. *Native Religions of North America*. San Francisco: Harper & Row, 1987.

Hutchins, Robert Maynard, and Mortimer Adler, eds. "East and West." In *Great Books of the Western World*, vol. 1, *The Great Conversation*. Chicago: Encyclopedia Britannica, 1952.

Irving, Washington. *A History of the Life and Voyages of Christopher Columbus*. Philadelphia: Carey, Lea & Blanchard Co.,1837.

BIBLIOGRAPHY

_____. *A History of the Life and Voyages of Christopher Columbus.* Edited by James W. Tuttleton. Boston: Twayne, 1987.

Jane, Cecil, ed. *The Four Voyages of Columbus* ("A History in Eight Documents, including five by Christopher Columbus, in the original Spanish with English translations"). New York: Dover Publications, 1988 (Reprint of the original 1929 and 1933 volumes of the Hakluyt Society).

Jennings, Francis. *The Ambiguous Iroquois Empire: The Covenant Chain of Indian Tribes with English Colonies from Its Beginning to the Lancaster Treaty of 1744.* New York: W. W. Norton, 1984.

Josephy, Alvin M., Jr., ed. *America in 1492: The World of the Indian Peoples Before the Arrival of Columbus.* New York: Knopf, 1992.

_____. *The Indian Heritage of America.* New York: Bantam, 1968.

Keegan, William F., "Beached in the Bahamas." *Archaeology* 45, no. 1 (January/February 1992).

Kehoe, Alice Beck. *North American Indians: A Comprehensive Account.* Englewood Cliffs, N.J.: Prentice-Hall, 1981.

Kellaway, William. *The New England Company, 1649–1776: Missionary Society to the American Indian.* London: Longmans, 1961.

Kenton, Edna, ed. *The Jesuit Relations and Allied Documents.* New York: A. Boni and C. Boni, 1925.

Knox, Bernard. "The Oldest Dead White European Males." *The New Republic*, 25 May 1992.

Koning, Hans. "Don't Celebrate 1492—Mourn It." *New York Times*, 14 August 1990.

_____. "Teach the Truth About Columbus." *Washington Post*, 3 September 1991.

Krauthammer, Charles. "Hail Columbus, Dead White Male." *Time*, 27 May 1991.

LaDuke, Winona. "We Are Still Here." *Sojourners* 20, no. 8 (October 1991).

Las Casas, Bartolomé de. *Historia de las Indias.* 3 vols. Mexico City: Fondo de cultura económica, 1951.

_____. *History of the Indies.* Translated and edited by Andrée Collard. New York: Harper & Row, 1971.

_____. *De unico vocationis modo.* In *Classics of Western Spirituality.* New York: Paulist Press, 1992.

León-Portilla, Miguel. *Aztec Thought and Culture.* Translated by Jack Emory Davis. Norman: University of Oklahoma Press, 1990.

187

Leo, John. "P.C. Follies." *U.S. News & World Report*, 27 January 1992.

Leo XIII, *Quarto abeunte saeculo*. In *The Papal Encyclicals*, edited by Claudia Carlen, vol. 2 (*1878–1903*). Raleigh, N.C.: McGrath Publishing, 1981.

Levenson, Jay A., ed. *Circa 1492: Art in the Age of Exploration*. Washington: National Gallery of Art, 1991.

López de Gómara, Francisco. *Primera Parte de la Historia General de las Indias*. Vol. 22. Madrid: Biblioteca de Autores Españoles, 1852.

McAllister, Bill. "Columbus Jubilee Panel Gets Few Answers." *Washington Post*, 22 November 1992.

MacLeish, William H. "1492 America: The Land Columbus Never Saw." *Smithsonian* 22, no. 8 (1991).

Martin, Joel S. *Sacred Revolt: The Muskogees Struggle for a New World*. Boston: Beacon Press, 1991.

Martinez, Demetria. "Bishop Challenges Knights To Drop Columbus." *National Catholic Reporter*, 25 August 1991.

Masters, Kim. "Some Might Call It Art . . . ." *Washington Post*, 9 February 1992.

Maxwell, James A., ed. *America's Fascinating Indian Heritage*. Pleasantville, N.Y.: Reader's Digest Association, 1978.

Maxwell, Kenneth. "The Mystery of Chico Mendes." *New York Review of Books*, 28 March 1991.

——————. "The Tragedy of the Amazon." *New York Review of Books*, 7 March 1991.

Moore, James T., *Indian and Jesuit: A Seventeenth-Century Encounter*. Chicago: Loyola University Press, 1982.

More, Thomas. *Utopia*. Translated by Paul Turner. New York: Penguin Books, 1961.

Morison, Samuel Eliot, *Admiral of the Ocean Sea*. 2 vols. Boston: Little, Brown & Co., 1942.

——————. *Christopher Columbus, Mariner*. New York: New American Library, 1956.

——————. *The European Discovery of America: The Northern Voyages*. New York: Oxford University Press, 1971.

——————, ed. and trans. *Journals and Other Documents on the Life and Voyages of Christopher Columbus*. New York: Heritage, 1963.

Muldoon, James. "The Columbus Quincentennial: Should Christians Celebrate It?" *America*, 27 October 1990.

Nash, Gary B., *Red, White, and Black: The Peoples of Early America*. Englewood Cliffs, N.J.: Prentice-Hall, 1974.

National Conference of Catholic Bishops (U.S.). "Heritage and Hope: Evangelization in America" (Pastoral Letter). Reprinted in *Origins* 20 (6 December 1990).

National Council for the Social Studies. *The Columbian Quincentenary: An Educational Opportunity*. October 1991.

National Council of the Churches of Christ in the U.S.A. *A Faithful Response to the 500th Anniversary of the Arrival of Christopher Columbus* (Resolution adopted by the Governing Board 17 May 1990). 475 Riverside Dr., New York, N.Y.

Newsweek, Special Issue, Fall/Winter 1991.

1992/Kairos USA. "A Call to the Work of Repentance." *Sojourners* 20, no. 8 (October 1991).

Noble, David W. *The Eternal Adam and the New World Garden*. New York: Grosset & Dunlap, 1968.

O'Gorman, Edmundo. *The Invention of America: An Inquiry into the Historical Nature of the New World and the Meaning of Its History*. Bloomington: Indiana University Press, 1961.

Pagden, Anthony. *The Fall of Natural Man: The American Indian and the Origins of Comparative Ethnology*. Cambridge: Cambridge University Press, 1982.

Paredes, Mario. "A Hispanic Reaction to the NCC." Northeast Hispanic Catholic Center, 1011 First Avenue, New York, N.Y., 25 July 1991. Reprinted in *Origins* 20 (16 August 1990).

Parkman, Francis. *The Jesuits in North America*. In *Parkman: France and England in North American*, vol. 1. New York: Library of America, 1983.

——————. *La Salle and the Discovery of the Great West*. In *Parkman: France and England in North America*, vol. 1. New York: Library of America, 1983.

Paz, Octavio. *Collected Poems, 1957–1987*. New York: New Directions, 1987.

——————. "Reflexiones de un intruso." *Vuelta*, January 1987.

Pearce, Roy Harvey. *Savagism and Civilization: A Study of the Indian and the American Mind*. Berkeley: University of California Press, 1988.

Peckham, Howard, and Charles Gibson, eds. *Attitudes of Colonial Powers Toward the American Indian*. Salt Lake City: University of Utah Press, 1969.

189

BIBLIOGRAPHY

Phillips, J. R. S., *The Medieval Expansion of Europe*. New York: Oxford University Press, 1988.

Phillips, William D., Jr., and Carla Rahn Phillips. *The Worlds of Christopher Columbus*. New York: Cambridge University Press, 1992.

Pidal, Ramón Menéndez. *El Padre Las Casas. Su doble personalidad.* Madrid: Espasa Calpe, 1963.

Poole, Stafford, Charles H. Lippy, and Robert Choquette, eds. *Christianity Comes to the Americas*. New York: Giniger Books, 1992.

Prucha, Francis Paul. *The Great Father: The United States Government and the American Indian*. 2 vols. Lincoln: University of Nebraska Press, 1984.

Reff, Daniel T. "Anthropological Analysis of Exploration Texts: Cultural Discourse and the Ethnological Import of Fray Marcos de Niza's Journey to Cibola." *The American Anthropologist*, no. 93 (September 1991).

Russell, Jeffrey Burton. *Inventing the Flat Earth: Columbus and Modern Historians*. New York: Praeger, 1991.

Sale, Kirkpatrick. *The Conquest of Paradise: Christopher Columbus and the Columbian Legacy*. New York: Knopf, 1990.

Salisbury, Neal. *Manitou and Providence: Indians, Europeans, and the Making of New England*, 1500–1643. New York: Oxford University Press, 1982.

Sanoff, Alvin P. "The Myths of Columbus" (Interview with Kirkpatrick Sale). *U.S. News & World Report*, 8 October 1990.

Schama, Simon. "They All Laughed at Christopher Columbus." *The New Republic*, 6–13 January 1992.

Schele, Linda, and David Freidel. *A Forest of Kings: The Untold Story of the Ancient Maya*. New York: William Morrow, 1990.

Schlesinger, Arthur M., Jr. "Four Days with Fidel: A Havana Diary." *New York Review of Books*, 26 March 1992.

——————. *The Disuniting of America: Reflections on a Multicultural Society*. New York: W. W. Norton, 1992.

Scott, James Brown. *The Spanish Origin of International Law*. Washington: Georgetown University Press, 1928.

"Separating the Man from the Myth." *Scholastic Update* 125, no. 2 (September 1991).

Silva Tena, Teresa. "El Sacrificio Humano En La *Apologética Historia*." *Historia Mexicana* 16 (1967).

Sokolov, Raymond. "Stop Knocking Columbus." *Newsweek*, Special Issue, Fall/Winter 1991.

190

——————. *Why We Eat What We Eat*. New York: Summit Books, 1992.

Soustelle, Jacques. *Daily Life of the Aztecs on the Eve of the Spanish Conquest*. Translated by Patrick O'Brien. Palo Alto: Stanford University Press, 1970.

Steinfels, Peter. "Beliefs." *New York Times*, 26 October 1991.

Sweet, Leonard I. "Christopher Columbus and the Millennial Vision of the New World." *The Catholic Historical Review* 72, no.3 (July 1986).

Taviani, Paolo Emilio. *Columbus: The Great Adventure*. Translated by Luciano F. Farina and Marc A. Beckwith. New York: Orion Books, 1991.

Thernstrom, Stephen. "The Columbus Controversy." *The American Educator* 16, no. 1 (Spring 1992).

Thwaite, Reuben Gold, ed. *The Jesuit Relations and Allied Documents*. 73 vols. Cleveland: Burrows Brothers, 1896–1901.

Todorov, Tzvetan. *The Conquest of America: The Question of the Other*. Translated by Richard Howard. New York: Harper & Row, 1985.

Tooker, Elizabeth. "The United States Constitution and the Iroquois League." In *The Invented Indian: Cultural Fictions and Government Policies*, edited by James Clifton. New Brunswick, N.J.: Transaction Books, 1990.

Trigger, Bruce G., ed. *Handbook of North American Indians*. 16 vols. Washington: Smithsonian Institution Press, 1978.

Tuck, Richard. *Natural Rights Theories: Their Origin and Development*. New York: Cambridge University Press, 1971.

Varela, C., ed. *Cristóbal Colón: Textos y documentos completos*. Madrid: 1984.

Vargas Llosa, Mario. "Questions of Conquest." *Harper's*, December 1990.

Vignaud, Henry. *Études critiques sur la vie de Christophe Colomb avant ses découvertes*. Paris: H. Welter, 1905.

Viola, Herman J., ed. and trans. *After Columbus: The Smithsonian Chronicle of the North American Indians*. Washington: Smithsonian Institution Press, 1991.

Viola, Herman J., and Carolyn Margolis, eds. *Seeds of Change: Five Hundred Years Since Columbus*. Washington: Smithsonian Institution Press, 1991.

Vitoria, Francisco de. *Political Writings*. Edited by Anthony Pagden and Jeremy Lawrence. New York: Cambridge University Press, 1991.

191

——————. *The Rights and Obligations of Indians and Spaniards in the New World.* Edited by Luciano Pereña Vincente. Salamanca and Washington: University of Salamanca and Catholic University of America, 1991.

Washburn, Wilcomb E. "History of Indian-White Relations." In *Handbook of North American Indians,* edited by Bruce G. Trigger, vol. 4. Washington: Smithsonian Institution Press, 1978.

——————. "The Meaning of 'Discovery' in the Fifteenth and Sixteenth Centuries." *The American Historial Review* 68 (October 1962).

——————. "Seventeenth-Century Indian Wars." In *Handbook of North American Indians,* edited by Bruce G. Trigger, vol. 15. Washington: Smithsonian Institution Press, 1978.

Watts, Pauline Moffitt. "Prophecy and Discovery: On the Spiritual Origins of Christopher Columbus's 'Enterprise of the Indies.' " *The American Historical Review* 90 (1985).

Weatherford, Jack. *Indian Givers.* New York: Crown, 1988.

Weissman, G. *They All Laughed at Christopher Columbus: Tales of Medicine and the Art of Discovery.* New York: Times Books, 1987.

Wilford, John Noble. *The Mysterious History of Columbus.* New York: Knopf, 1991.

Wills, Garry. "Goodbye, Columbus." *New York Review of Books,* 22 November 1990.

——————. "Man of the Year." *New York Review of Books,* 21 November 1991.

Winsor, Justin. *Christopher Columbus, and How He Received and Imparted the Spirit of Discovery.* Cambridge, Mass.: Cambridge University Press, 1891.

Woodward, C. Vann. *The Old World's New World.* New York: Oxford University Press, 1991.

Index of Names

Index

INDEX

This book was typeset in Bembo (text) and Weiss (display) by Coghill Composition Company of Richmond, Virginia. It was printed by Edwards Brothers of Ann Arbor, Michigan.